Ok
Paren

PRACTICAL HEALTH

Okay Parenting

MAVIS KLEIN

PIATKUS

Copyright © 1991 by Mavis Klein

First published in 1991 by
Judy Piatkus (Publishers) Ltd
5 Windmill Street, London W1P 1HF

British Library Cataloguing in Publication Data

Klein, Mavis
    Okay parenting: A psychological handbook for parents.
    I. Title
    155.6

    ISBN 0–7499–1064–X
    ISBN 0–7499–1058–5 pbk

Edited by Susan Fleming
Designed by Sue Ryall

Typeset in Linotron Times by
Phoenix Photosetting, Chatham, Kent
Printed and bound in Great Britain by
Billing and Sons Ltd, Worcester

CONTENTS

INTRODUCTION

I have written this book out of my own experiences of being a mother (for thirty years), a psychotherapist (for fifteen years), and a grandmother (for five years). I am – now – very confident in each of these roles, and it is my great wish to share this confidence with other parents so that you can benefit from my experience and learning.

This reassuring and helpful handbook covers everyday situations faced by parents where a little psychological insight and understanding will help the child grow up balanced, healthy and independent, and help you, the parent, deal with 'problems' in a confident and effective way. I accept that my opinions and attitudes may occasionally come across as exaggerated or dogmatic. They are the result of fifteen years spent working as a psychotherapist and dealing with situations just like those in this book. Any dogmatism is the price I am willing to pay for the confidence of my convictions.

In nearly all the entries, the opinions and attitudes expressed rest on the received wisdom of the psychoanalytic view of child development (based on the genius of Freud), combined with the wisdom of the theory of Transactional Analysis (based on the genius of Eric Berne). The gloss of my own wide experience is added to many entries, for which I claim full credit and responsibility.

The first demand made, therefore, of each reader of this book, is that you accept without scepticism the fundamental assumption of Psychoanalysis – that is, that the unconscious mind exists. Thereafter you must accept that the unconscious mind covertly influences a great deal of what we consciously feel, do, and think; that it very often expresses powerful motives in us that are contrary to the motives of our conscious minds; and that the experiences of our earliest years of life profoundly determine virtually all that we experience in the rest our lives. Once these assumptions are accepted – and they are at the core of most psychotherapeutic practice the world over – the quintessential importance of the psychological relationship between parents and children will be much more fully appreciated and understood.

As well as implying enormous responsibility, there is no greater power on earth than that automatically bestowed on people when they (choose to) become parents: the hand that rocks the cradle rules the world. Furthermore, becoming a parent is the natural final stage in functional maturation.

Introduction

That is, it bestows on us, willy-nilly, the *joy of love* – willingly making another person's well-being and happiness as important (if not more important) than our own. People who do not have children are hard-pressed to find for themselves commitments that will guarantee them the complete fulfilment in life that only comes from passionately serving others' as well as our own needs and desires. Whereas, for as long as they are alive, parents are automatically granted this profound satisfaction by the mere existence of their children.

Parenthood is a constant tightrope act, a creative struggle to find and maintain the 'just-right' balance between encouragement and constraint, throughout the ever-changing developmental needs of children. As the 17th-century philosopher, John Locke, put it so beautifully:

> '*To avoid the danger that is on either hand is the great art; and he that has found a way how to keep up a child's spirit, easy, active and free and yet, at the same time, to restrain him from many things he has a mind to, and to drive him to things that are uneasy to him; he, I say, that knows how to reconcile these seeming contradictions has in my opinion got the true secret of education.*'

We also have to accept that in our creative struggles in rearing our children – as in all creative endeavours – we are not 'perfect', but humanly frail. While we consciously determine not to commit on our children the sins that our parents inflicted on us, we will inevitably – consciously or unconsciously – commit other sins, which our children, in turn, will determinedly avoid in the rearing of their children. And what of the genetically determined characteristics in both ourselves and our children that so obviously limit our own abilities to be all that we might want to be to our children, and limit our children's abilities to benefit from what we are able and willing to offer them?

In everything we do in our lives, and probably especially in the task of being a parent, we are bound to accept our impotence as well as our power, our badness as well as our goodness, our failures as well as our successes. And, ironically, it is in being 'good enough' rather than 'perfect' parents that we love our children best, because only by eventually perceiving their parents as good and powerful and loveworthy *and* humanly flawed, are grown-up children able to attain full self-esteem and confidence in the face of their awareness of their own flawed nature. Some of the most frightened and unhappy grown-ups are so by virtue of having been imbued with the idea of their parents' unassailable 'perfection'.

Yet, despite all its headaches and heartaches, for the vast majority of people, parenthood is still the most worthwhile task in the world and potentially the profoundest and most unassailable meaning we may give to our lives. I hope that this book will help you in achieving the greater fulfilment of your parenthood through the awareness I offer you to add to your love. If you know what you are doing and why, you will not only enjoy it more, but will carry it out with greater success.

The first section of this book is an overview of the broad psychological stages through which all human beings develop from birth to young adulthood. It is based on the theories of Freud and Berne and you may find it gives you additional insight and understanding on aspects of child behaviour and development. Some of the concepts may sound extreme but do not be put off by them; they are the basis for much work in child and family psychology. I include them in order for you to understand more fully the advice I give in the A–Z section.

The broad stages of development are Birth to Six Months, Six Months to One Year, One to Three, Three to Six, Six to Twelve, Twelve to Sixteen, and Sixteen and Up.

The second section of this book is an alphabetically compiled compendium of topics concerning specific issues that may arise in any or all of the general stages of development. Each entry is dealt with as concisely or as lengthily as I have felt necessary to delineate the general nature of the issue and its appropriate handling; but, for each topic, reference is made to other, related topics, to help you home in on the precise issue that concerns you. Where necessary I also recommend reference to the relevant general stage of development, in order to place the symptom and its significance in its appropriate context. For example, transient stealing in adolescence is far less significant than it is at age eight; and school phobia is far less significant at age five than it is at twelve. Any symptom – be it a normal variation of personality or a sign of significant psychological dis-ease – should always be thought about in terms specific to a particular child at a particular time in a particular context, rather than be presumed to have a singular meaning in itself.

I am grateful to my editors for the many topics they drew to my attention, and I hope that the consistent underlying philosophy, informing all that I have to say, will be extended by you to any topics I may yet have overlooked. For, although this book is about the specific psychological relationship of parents to their children, I hope that you will also find in it many insights that facilitate your effectiveness in your dealings with people in general, particularly in interactions with intimate others, *besides* your children. However, it always needs to be borne in mind that the relationship between parents and children is uniquely asymmetrical: *parents are utterly responsible for their children, children are not at all responsible for their parents.*

Mavis Klein,
London, November 1990

PART ONE

The Seven Stages of Childhood

BIRTH TO SIX MONTHS

New-born babies express with unselfconscious explicitness the core truth about all human beings, namely that we are utterly self-seeking and care for nothing and nobody as much as our own self-preservation in the first place, and the immediate gratification of our every desire and impulse in the second place. Those of us who are not very young babies realize that we cannot fulfil our selfish wants without the help of others – who are also, at core, utterly self-ish – and so we know we have to give them some of what they want in order for them to be willing to give us some of what we want. For-tunately for new-born babies, 'the maternal instinct' by and large ensures that mothers are uniquely willing, at this time, to be genuinely altruistic in fulfilling all of their baby's desires to the best of their ability, without considering the fulfilment of their own desires or needs.

In the beginning, it may be inferred, our first cry, on being born, is the expression of our first experience of (painful) unfulfilled desire. We have emerged from the condition of having all our needs met without having to do anything; now we have to breathe and cry. We have no concept of ourselves or of anyone else; the universe and ourselves are one. The only distinctions we make are of total satis-faction – in which case we are either feeding or asleep – or of total pain – in which case the universe consists wholly of our screaming desire for food or the elimination of other bodily pain.

For new-born babies, the loving skin-to-skin contact given them by their parents is as vital to their survival as food, and most parents instinctively give their babies this, and most babies grow and thrive. A contented baby held lovingly in its mother's arms is the epitome of bliss, to which state of being we all long to return (and come closest to in the ecstasy of sexual orgasm with a partner whom we passionately desire).

The unconditional, self-abnegating love that a healthy mother gives her new-born baby effectively says to the baby, 'I love you because you are you, irrespective of anything you do to please or displease me.' This is the basis of the child experiencing *trust in the essential benevolence of the universe*, which is the necessary pre-condition for the healthy progress of the child through all the other developmental stages to maturity. All babies, between birth and six months, are universally demanding, completely self-centred, spontaneous, honest, and uninhibited. The fully accepting responsiveness that parents exhibit to their baby at this stage will ensure in their child a lifelong capacity, spontaneously and joyously, to express his or her emotions and desires.

SIX MONTHS TO ONE YEAR

In the second half of the first year of life the child begins to 'know' things in a quite explicit way, and he is preeminently motivated to know more and more through his exploration of the environment. Exhausting as his new-found mobility is for his mother, it is crucially important for the child's healthy development at this stage for him to be physically constrained only as often as is absolutely necessary for his safety. Remove your own precious things out of his reach for a few months (until, by about one year of age, he is capable of understanding 'No' and, indeed, needs to learn to respond adaptively to your prohibitions), rather than lock him in a playpen. The child's exploratory drive from six to twelve months of age is the foundation of his lifelong capacity for joyous play and creativity, and inhibiting him now will permanently inhibit his spontaneity and his creativity. (It has actually been shown that children of about seven or eight who were, as infants, regularly put in a playpen, are less competent at reading and writing than those who were not so imprisoned.) This is the stage when parents' essential responsibility is to give their child permission to *play and explore*, and these permissions, if granted now, will result in their enhanced pleasurable expression by the child throughout his or her life.

The child now knows he is a separate being from his mother and is poignantly aware of his dependence on her for his survival. He now experiences his first real fear – that his mother will abandon him – manifest as 'separation anxiety', which reaches its peak between about eight and ten months of age. To make his fear of abandonment tolerable, towards the end of the first year of his life the child learns to enjoy playing 'peek-a-boo', through which he pretends his mother has left him, but makes her come back, at his bidding, when he takes his hands away from his eyes. The tension of his fear is dissolved in the ensuing laughter. This game continues to be played by human beings throughout their lives in the thrills they get from *pretend* life-threatening experiences, such as riding the big-dipper.

ONE TO THREE

In the interests of the child's safety and socialization, and the preservation of the parents' sanity, it becomes necessary, from about one year of age, to inhibit and constrain some of the child's natural impulses with a large number of *'Don'ts'*. These 'Don'ts' have to be imposed both verbally and physically by parents on a child of this age because the child has neither the knowledge nor the care and consideration for himself or others that would enable him voluntarily, for example, not to tear his parents' books up, not to scream for what he wants, and not to jump off a sixth-floor balcony. So at this stage parents are bound to inculcate *fear of retribution* into their child, with sufficient power that the child internalizes their punitive wrath in his own mind.

An angry look or forceful bodily removal of the child, accompanied by 'Don't touch the stove', 'Don't pull the cat's tail', 'Don't scream', 'Don't pick your nose', 'Don't take . . .', 'Don't hurt . . .' quickly become a part of the child's own mind, after which he automatically responds to these prohibitions even when his parents are not around. If he disobeys a prohibition, he no longer needs Mother or Father to stop him or give him an angry look; *he stops himself, by giving himself the appropriately inculcated bad feeling* previously imposed on him by his parents, and may even remonstrate aloud with himself, such as by shaking his head and saying 'No, no' by the time he gets within two feet of the stove, the cat's tail, etc. This simple, mindless obedience is the precursor of the morality (which develops from three to six years of age) which will later inhibit his self-destructive and anti-social impulses with *justifications* that he will then be capable of understanding due to his also developed reasoning ability.

Thus the one to three year old is, of necessity, constrained by punishment and the fear of it. *The impulses in the child that are inhibited by the 'Don'ts' imposed on him at this time will, by and large, be inhibited in him for the rest of his life.* Any transgression of these inhibitions will make him feel very bad indeed about himself – also for the rest of his life.

So it is of the utmost importance at this stage of a child's development for parents scrupulously to monitor their own motives whenever they impose a 'Don't', and to limit them to those that are truly necessary for the preservation of the child's safety and basic social acceptability. Many parents impose a large number of 'Don't' on their child that serve no positive purposes at all, but are imposed merely through the parents' laziness in choosing expediency over more effortful and positive ways of protecting and socializing the child. The child pays for such laziness in his parents with the pain of unnecessary inhibitions for the rest of his life.

Furthermore, parents may transmit 'Don'ts' to their child that represent their own unnecessary, painful 'hang-ups'. These 'Don'ts' are usually transmitted covertly and non-verbally (and so more powerfully, because actions speak louder than words). For example, a young child pushed away when he tries to clamber on to his father's knee probably receives the inhibitory message, 'Don't be close', and is always likely to have difficulty in forming intimate relationships. An embarrassed look on the face of a mother whose child says, 'I hate my brother' is likely to be received as 'Don't express bad feelings', and the child is likely to be rigidly polite and inauthentic in his emotional expressiveness for the rest of his life. An angry look given to a child who praises himself for something he has done well, is usually taken by the child to mean, 'Don't succeed', and he is likely chronically to judge himself a failure, irrespective of his actual accomplishments. And a disgusted look given to a child who has accidentally soiled his pants most likely means, 'Don't feel good about yourself', and this child will grow up to be a perfectionist who chronically feels guilty about his own behaviour and is critically blemishing of other people as well.

While it is probably the case that only a minority of parents scrupulously and self-consciously seek to avoid passing on their own hang-ups to their child, all normally loving parents instinctively make an effort more often to protect and socialize their children by rewards rather than punishment. Many – but perhaps too few! – parents realize that, for example, 'Mummy is cross with you when you make a lot of noise' will as surely create a grown-up woman who *is* noisy (*and* feels bad about herself for this) as 'What a good girl being so quiet' will create a grown-up woman who is generally quite (*and* feels good about herself for this). So always, if at all possible, at this most receptive stage of development, mould a child's behaviour by praise not blame, by 'Do's' not 'Don'ts', by reward not punishment. It may take a little extra effort to translate an impulse to 'No' into a somewhat more complicated encouragement to do something to which you can say yes, but the effect on your child will be enormously enhancing of her self-esteem – now and for the rest of her life.

Between the ages of one and three, alongside the crucially significant *inhibitions* that are developed in the child, the child's reasoning ability is also emerging and growing, and is expressed in the acquisition of objective knowledge and skills. The abundant praise that loving parents normally give their child for every new skill or piece of knowledge he exhibits, not only makes the child feel good about himself, but also reinforces the child's impulses for knowledge and competence, and enhances his ability, *for the rest of his life, to enjoy activities that do not necessitate interactions with other people*. This 'self-sufficiency' is, of course, of the utmost value when, for any reason, throughout life, others are not available to provide mental or emotional stimulation. From one to three, growing self-sufficient competency is largely manifest in practical skills, such as in the child fully feeding himself, building a tower of blocks, blowing his nose, pouring water from one container to another, and, above all else, in the acquisition of language.

The child is now aware that his parents' (and others') loving approval of him is by no means unconditional. He knows that he must be 'good' to get the approval he wants. But he does not yet have a moral code with which to justify his 'good' behaviour. Notwithstanding any apparently 'caring' or 'sharing' behaviour he may display or words he may utter, these are actually only mechanically imitative of his parents.

From one to three, the orientation of the child's self-esteem is centred around the *fear of retribution*, his defence against which is obedience.

THREE TO SIX

Between the ages of three and six every girl falls in love with her father, wants to get rid of her mother in order to possess him, and has to come to terms with the realities that she can neither possess her father nor get rid of her mother. She is forced to compromise her desires and, ideally, she reconciles herself to her frustration by deciding, 'When I grow up I am going to be a lady like Mummy and marry a man like Daddy.'

Between the ages of three and six every boy falls in love with his mother, wants to get rid of his father in order to possess her, and has to come to terms with the realities that he can neither possess his mother nor get rid of his father. He is forced to compromise his desires and, ideally, he reconciles himself to his frustration by deciding, 'When I grow up I am going to be a man like Daddy and marry a lady like Mummy.'

The parents' roles at this stage of the child's development demand that they, too, express the best possible *compromise* between reinforcing the child's sexual self-esteem while denying it the specific gratification it presently seeks. The boy wants to feel that his mother loves him more than she loves her father; the girl wants to feel that her father loves her more than he loves her mother. It is imperative that the child be defeated in this aim. The child experiencing him- or herself to be the victor in this battle is one of the greatest tragedies that can occur with respect to his or her subsequent lifelong ability to form satisfying relationships with the opposite sex and, indeed, to establish and maintain a satisfying self-image and satisfying attitudes to the world and life in general.

The Oedipal battle, played out by Mother, Father, and child is overwhelmingly *the* most deterministic experience in the formation of our individuality and our relationship propensities and needs for the rest of our lives. *For essentially healthy functioning throughout his or her life, the Oedipal battle must be lost by the child.*

On the other hand, the subsequent healthy sexual self-esteem of the child also depends on the receipt of a loving response from the opposite-sexed parent to his or her crypto-sexual overtures. A girl profoundly needs her father, at this stage, to express admiration for her looks and her clothes and to pay homage to her sweetness and her charm; and a boy profoundly needs his mother, at this stage, to express admiration for his attempts to impress her with his strength and bravery and power. Thus, when Daddy comes home from work and his daughter rushes to kiss him before Mummy can, a loving mother understandingly allows this to happen, and a loving father plays with his daughter for a while before firmly telling her that it is time for them to stop playing because he wants to talk to and cuddle Mummy. And when Daddy comes home from work, a loving mother insistently pushes her son away from her, telling him she wants to be with Daddy now that he has come home, but that, after dinner *Daddy* will play with him.

From this prototypical scenario it is evident that girls' and boys' experiences of the Oedipal stage are not symmetrical. Both girls and boys needed to be granted some gratification of their possessive attachment to their opposite-sexed parent, while at the same time being somewhat coercively propelled into relinquishing that possessiveness in favour of modelling themselves, by identification, on the attributes of their same-sexed parent. But both boys and girls typically spend much more time with their mothers than their fathers, so a boy's possessive attachment to his mother is likely to be greater than a girl's possessive attachment to her father. In the ordinary course of events, a boy has to struggle harder to free himself from his mother and attain his sexual autonomy than a girl has to struggle to free herself from her father and attain her sexual autonomy. (When, for whatever reason, a boy is overwhelmed by his symbiotic attachment to his mother it *may* account for his becoming homosexual. And the generally easier task for a girl of separating from her father may, to some extent, account for the greater prevalence of male over female homosexuality.)

What emerges out of all of this is the child's character, which, broadly speaking, is his or her morality and ability appropriately both to control and nurture his or her own and others' impulses (aggressive and sexual) in the light of *recognition of the need to compromise between his or her own and others' desires*. The child is now able appropriately sometimes to feel responsible or guilty, and sometimes to blame others. The child is also now capable of sharing and caring responses towards other people, and a considerable degree of self-discipline in maintaining his or or her own general well-being. Now he understands the 'reason' for many of the prohibitions that were imposed on him from one to three which, at that time, he was made non-comprehendingly simply to obey. Now he fears the retribution of his own conscience as much as the withdrawal of love of his mother and father.

Also at this time, with his or her newly-acquired moral code, the child's behaviour is broadened by virtue of *added flexibility*. For example, as a two-year-old he may have been made to accept that he was *never* allowed to eat chocolate after 7 p.m., and he fearfully obeyed this prohibition just because Mummy or Daddy said so. Now, as a six-year-old, he understands the *general principle* that sugar causes tooth decay, which must be protected against by toothbrushing, so he may quite self-righteously choose to eat some chocolate after 7 p.m. (at which time he cleaned his teeth), so long as he cleans them again after eating the chocolate. A two-year-old may imitatively 'share' some chocolate with her dolly and 'eat it for her', but a six-year old is capable of truly sharing a bar of chocolate with a friend. And a six-year-old is, in principle, capable of understanding such concepts as 'a white lie', where a smaller 'good' is sacrificed to a larger one.

The child now knows that 'giving' as well as 'taking' is inevitably demanded of him if he is to receive the loving attention he wants from others. From now on, he or she is implicitly aware that *tenderness and aggression* have to be balanced in the expression of his or her desire for intimacy with others. Unresolved symbiotic attachment to the opposite-sexed parent will incline the child, throughout his life, to too much tenderness, that is, to an under-developed ability to express lusty sexual desire and eroticism. Undissolved symbiotic attachment to the same-sexed parent will incline the child, throughout his life, to too much aggression in his or her sexual relationships, that is, an under-developed ability to love him-or herself and, therefore, others.

From three to six, at a deep level, the self-esteem of a boy is centrally threatened by the *fear of castration*, and the self-esteem of a girl is centrally threatened by the *fear of being undesirable*. The defence against these fears is the child's willingness to *compromise* between his or her desires and the desires of others.

From the evidence of children brought up in orphanages or communes or in the absence of one of their parents, it would seem that the Oedipus complex is, at least partly, biologically precipitated into the experience of three- to six-year-old children, irrespective of external reality. And any child in our culture who has somehow managed to 'bypass' the Oedipal battle will inevitably be severely handicapped throughout his or her life by the gaps in his experience that should be filled with beliefs about a multitude of experiences (including aggression, love, blame, guilt, envy, jealousy, rivalry, ambition, power, and revenge), the knowledge of which is learned through the Oedipal battle and constitutes *emotional literacy*. The experience of the Oedipus complex is crucial in determining the qualities of the child's subsequent relationships and his or her attitudes to nearly everything else in life as well, and – from my experience as a psychotherapist – I can vouch for the fact that deviations from the norm of the eternal triangle of mother, father, and child are likely to overwhelm in significance all other experiences combined in the child's development from birth to maturity.

SIX TO TWELVE

This period of development is called 'latency' in psychoanalytic theory, because sexuality (which Psychoanalysis understands to be the basic life-force in us throughout life) is temporarily suppressed in favour of intellectual development, and social learning through identification with same-sexed peers. It is as if, recoiling bruised from his or her rejection in love (from three to six), the child now seeks compensation in *control over external reality* through the acquisition of knowledge and competence and growing identification with the ways of being and doing of his or her same-sexed parent and same-sexed peers. The pain of love is defended against with a 'yuk' attitude towards the opposite sex, although the suppression of the heterosexual impulse is far from complete, and 'I'll show you mine if you show me yours' is a popular and frequent intermission in the aggressive hostility between the sexes that characterizes this stage of development.

Much of the child's healthy development is now in the hands of her teachers, who instruct her and reinforce the culturally demanded skills of literacy, numeracy, and sociability. Subsidiarily, parents typically expand their child's knowledge and interests in the world at large by taking her on outings, arranging swimming and music lessons, etc.

In general, the child is a much *less emotional* being now than she ever has been before or ever will be again, and is therefore less vulnerable than at any other stage of her development to traumatization by contingent stresses that may beset her or her family. So now is the best time – if needs be – for parents to separate and divorce, because the child is more able now than at other stages of her development to 'take it in her stride'. (Contrary to much popular misunderstanding, a child's emotional vulnerability to her parents' divorce – or other stressful circumstances – does *not* decrease uniformly with age: twelve to sixteen is probably the most vulnerable age of all.)

But turning away from the quest for (painful) sexual love in favour of autonomous control of the external environment exacts *its* fearful price, too. The quest for omnipotence is poignantly linked to the awareness of our mortality, and the six- to twelve-year old child realistically knows about death in general and that she, too, must one day die. Her fear of death may be a closely guarded secret, observable only in the many obsessive-compulsive rituals and magical rites she surrounds herself with in her fearful bid to 'stop bad things happening'. More defiantly, she may revel in war games, horror stories, and violent films – the more gruesome the better – although girls are more inclined (in accordance with their anatomy?) to prefer psychological to physical viciousness. However, these attitudes are only partly successful defences against the fear of death, which is the greatest threat to the child's confidence at this time. Cynicism and depression are more often experienced by a child during this stage of development than is commonly realized. But if parents themselves have a wholesomely positive attitude to life they need not fear that their child's transient negativity will be lasting.

TWELVE TO SIXTEEN (PUBERTY)

At puberty the child is suddenly overwhelmed by a biologically-determined surge of sexual-aggressive energy, and manifestly demands its fulfilment as if in infancy again. But he or she is not an infant and cannot escape the established realities of his conditioning, his reasoning, and his morality. Much as he might wish, he cannot escape into the naïvety of infancy, but nor are his reasoning and his morality powerful enough to contain the insistent demands of his libido. What he does to help himself is to revert to the conditioning he experienced from one to three and turn it upside-down. In response to all the 'Don'ts' to which he was, from one to three, essentially obedient, he is now essentially rebellious. Discounting as far as he possibly can all the good sense of his later-developed reasoning and morality, he justifies, as far as he possibly can, the expression of his sexual and aggressive impulses with the *obverse* of all that he was taught from one to three; all the 'Don'ts' now become 'Do's'. He behaves rudely, inconsiderately, and often with scant regard for his own safety and well-being. He is much less trustworthy, less reliable, and less sensible than he was when he was ten. He treats his parents with the disdain, contempt and anger due to them as the gaolers he perceives them to be.

Loving parents know that all this is the natural and healthy way for their child to be at this stage of his or her development, and that their task is to walk the tightrope of tolerating just so much and no more. (Any parents who, in comparing notes with other parents of pubescent children smugly insist that *their* children are 'no trouble at all' are actually revealing that their children are *seriously pathologically repressed*. Sooner or later these children will be beset with incapacitating psychological handicaps in their grown-up lives, for which their parents will rightly be held responsible.) But since the child now utterly disregards their approval, parents have to struggle to find sanctions they can effectively impose on him. Often the granting and withholding of money – which the child now explicitly

15

wants and needs for libidinous display purposes – is the only power parents maintain over their child at this time, and they may use it to manipulate him into minimal acquiescence to their demands of him. Appeals to the child's 'better nature' are a waste of time; he has virtually no 'better nature' now.

To a large extent puberty is a recapitulation and honing of the one- to three-year-old stage. At that pre-Oedipal stage, obedience was, for the child, generally a small price to pay for the maintenance of the love of his parents, who overwhelmingly provided him with his greatest interpersonal gratifications. Now, post-Oedipally *and* with his newly-acquired and overwhelmingly powerful genital sexual impulses, his parents no longer fulfil his most imperative needs. Thus, at this time, it is as if he regrets having 'given' (in his obedience) to the wrong people, and he seeks to correct this 'mistake' by rebellion against them. Not until he has proudly and happily established a secure sexual relationship for himself will his parents cease to be the *threat to his autonomy and sexual gratification* that they now seem to him to be. Then, ideally, his relationship to them will revert to the pre-Oedipal quality of asexual mutual love they all once knew. For the time being, the child must struggle through his confusion while his parents poignantly accept the present necessity for things to be as they are, and it is of the utmost importance that parents never express – nor even allow themselves to experience – 'hurt feelings' for the insulting and hateful attributions the child so often hurls at them at this time. Parents feeling 'hurt by' their child (at *any* stage of his or her development) can only induce unhealthy guilt in the child and, at this stage in particular, the child needs to be given permission to feel and to express hostility and rebellion which he now *needs* to do for his healthy development.

This does not, of course, mean that parents set no controlling limits on their child's behaviour or speech. Their child needs to perceive them both as *emotionally invulnerable* to his assaults on them, *and more powerful* than he is in determining the limits of his rudeness, rebellion, etc.

Transitionally – in our culture – before the child is mature enough *emotionally* to be encouraged to express his full genital sexuality, he finds a temporary salve to his self-esteem through exaggerated identification with his same-sexed peer group. This is comparatively easy for him because it is a natural extension of the same-sexed friendships he became competent in during latency, although this may now precipitate some homosexual impulses, which may be expressed physically (but often only emotionally, especially in girls).

SIXTEEN AND UP (ADOLESCENCE)

Adolescence is the period roughly spanning the ages sixteen to twenty-one, when parents are called on to fulfil their final essential role in the rearing of their children to independent adulthood. At this stage parents are beginning to breathe a sigh of relief that their turbulent, rude, rebellious, utterly selfish, amoral, dare-devil, couldn't-care-less twelve to sixteen year old is apparently going to be human after all.

Now, although in many respects things are 'getting better' in the family, and the child is exhibiting a modicum of good manners and some absorbing educational or other interest of which the parents basically approve, emotionally the child is still very much at odds with his or her parents. The Oedipal battle of the three- to six-year-old stage (of angry rivalry with the same-sexed parent for the love of the opposite-sexed parent) is now being replayed in order to complete the moral development of the child. At that earlier Oedipal stage the child was bound, healthily, to lose the battle for supremacy over the same-sexed parent and to feel rejected by the opposite-sexed parent. Now he needs to express his or her symbolic revenge on them both by himself rejecting the love of his opposite-sexed parent and angrily competing with his or her same-sexed parent for power and desirability. Thus, when both sides of the coin have been expressed, the child achieves moral maturity by becoming realistically capable of assessing himself and other people as sometimes 'good' and sometimes 'bad', sometimes culpable and sometimes innocent, sometimes right and sometimes wrong.

Wise and loving parents, secure in their own sexual and other self-esteem, collude with their child's healthy aim to separate from his or her sexual-emotional bonding to them at this stage. Incestuous impulses are felt and must be fought against by both parents and child. An opposite-sexed parent needs insistently *not* to talk about sexual matters to the child and to appreciate and welcome (rather than 'feel hurt' by) the child's expression of revulsion towards intimate contact between them. A same-sexed parent needs constantly to express admiration for the child's accomplishments and attractiveness, and to play down his or her own accomplishments and attractiveness.

However, in general moral matters, the child still needs his parents' loving control for the attainment of a well-enough developed set of functioning moral standards. He needs to go out into the world armed with a set of beliefs and values that will stand him in good stead until such time, as an adult established in the larger world, he may safely and assuredly *modify* those parental values in the light of changing realities in his own life.

At this stage the child knows that he still needs his parents to help him achieve this final stage in his functional maturation. But because of his struggle against incestuous desire for his opposite-sexed parent and his rivalry with his same-sexed parent – which prompt him to keep a comfortable distance from both of them – he is resentful of his continuing need of them, and so has to camouflage his need. With his now well-developed capacity for logical reasoning, he initiates arguments with his parents, launching a two-pronged attack on their reasoning and their values, with consummate debating skill and sophistry. But *covertly* he is begging them confidently to *lay down the law* from their own confident value system, so that he may firmly internalize their values and achieve confidence in himself. The last thing he really wants is for them to crumple under his attacks, although manifestly this seems to be his aim.

At first, most parents are inclined to fall into the adolescent's trap by responding to his logical attacks on their beliefs and principles with their own logical reasoning, and the child often 'wins' the argument. But, in due course, appropriately wise and loving parents realize what is going on and accept this final essential responsibility of child-rearing, which is insistently to assert the validity of their own beliefs and to discount the relevance of any 'facts' or logic to the contrary. Internally, the child is profoundly grateful, but is unlikely to show it, and will certainly not explicitly express thanks to his parents for it until he is confidently established in adult life and has probably become a good and loving parent himself. Then the mutual, safe, asexual love between parents and child, last experienced in the first three years of the child's life, is finally restored.

PART TWO

A to Z
of Parenting

Abandonment

The complete helplessness of a new-born baby means that it inevitably dies within, at most, a few days if abandoned. Only gradually, over about the first twenty years of life, does a human being become self-sufficient enough that its physical survival is not threatened by being abandoned by its caretakers.

Throughout our lives we feel our *psychological* survival to be dependent on the reciprocal caring for us of the people we deeply love. The death of a loved person is the most complete abandonment we can experience, and – at least temporarily – shatters our self-confidence and our love of life, no matter how physically self-sufficient and grown-up we may be.

When we are children, the utter confidence that parents imbue in us that we will *never* be abandoned is the single most necessary factor ensuring our psychological well-being. This security makes us confident of our own *goodness* and, consequently, enables us to love life itself, which is the necessary basis for our being able to love other people. To threaten or actually to abandon a child is the cruellest psychological trauma that a parent can inflict and it almost inevitably results in the child having a lifelong overwhelming fear of retribution. If the child believes its abandonment has occurred because of its own *intrinsic badness*, so it is unable to love itself, life, or other people.

(See also **Death, Divorce, Fear, Rejection, Security, Separation.**)

Accidents

All children – and grown-ups – have accidents sometimes that damage their bodies and/or property. 'Accident-prone' people can be inferred to have an unconscious motive to hurt themselves or damage property, which motive should be understood and overcome. In general, the underlying motive for a child's accident-proneness is likely to be either a bid to get more loving attention from his parents than he normally gets, or a bid to be more stimulated by his environment, which prompts him to exciting activities with unpredictable outcomes. Both of these motives are, in themselves, wholesome, but the fulfilment of them by means of accidents is not. If your child is accident-prone, see if you can find an obvious cause for his needing more loving attention than he is getting, or for his needing more physical (or mental) challenges from his environment.

Chronic clumsiness, leading to frequent minor accidents, often reflects a child's (or grown-up's) low self-esteem. It is as if, in her clumsiness, the child is saying, 'Look how incompetent I am compared with Mummy/Daddy/ brother/sister . . .' Do not shout at or otherwise punish a child for her clumsiness, because this only confirms her low self-esteem and so actually reinforces her tendency to clumsiness. Instead, as far as possible, be nonchalant about her maladroitness, while finding subtle ways of getting her to do things competently and well and giving her abundant praise for doing so.

(See also **Comforting, Illness, Punishment.**)

Addiction

All human beings are capable of becoming addicted to certain substances. Nobody who smokes cigarettes needs telling what horrible slavery it is to be an addict. This slavery is, of course, avoidable by never beginning to smoke or to experiment with any other known addictive substance.

Children may smoke or not smoke in imitation or defiance of their parents. And there is considerable evidence that some people are genetically more pre-disposed to becoming addicts than others.

Altogether the causes of an addiction are usually complex and the cure equally complex. The best that parents can do is to warn their children to avoid behaviour that may lead to the unhappiness that addictions bring with them.

(See also **Drug-abuse.**)

Adoption

It is natural and inevitable that adopted children be curious about their biological parents. Yet it is also natural that they tend to feel guilty about this curiosity, which they believe implies disloyalty towards their loving, adoptive parents. The onus is on the adoptive parents explicitly to relieve the child of this guilt and to encourage him or her in early adult life to make contact (if at all possible) with his or her biological parents. Without the fullest possible knowledge of his or her biological parents, a child will incorporate them in his mind as ambivalently frightening and irresistibly attractive beings. These fantasies can interfere with and sabotage his ability to form lasting intimate relationships in adult life. He will metaphorically replay his confused feelings of divided loyalty, which is likely to be expressed in repeated unhappy patterns of intimacy, such as marrying one woman or man, only to find him- or herself desperately in love with some other, unattainable woman or man.

'Good' versus 'bad' is the most fundamental construct in the human mind, and all children have to go through stages in their development of seeing their parents as 'all-good' or 'all-bad' in the process whereby they achieve a mature understanding that 'there is good and bad in everybody'. While most loving adoptive parents instinctively refrain from defining the child's biological parents as 'bad' to the child, I believe it is also mistaken for adoptive parents to 'make excuses for' and define the biological parents as totally 'good' to the child. Rather they need openly to present to the child all the facts they know about the biological parents, in a morally neutral way, and encourage the child to make contact with them if possible. The child's innate psychological programming will then complete the process healthily, and the adoptive parents will be loved more rather than less by the child for their willingness to let the child relate to his or her biological parents as well as themselves.

(See also **Good and Evil**.)

Aggression

Aggression, together with sexuality, constitutes the energetic life-force in us all. It needs to find legitimate expression – not repression

– in activities ranging from hammer toys to football, to its most disguised and 'civilized' forms such as conducting an orchestra or being 'political' in one's job. For hormonal reasons, boys (and men), along with the males of other species, typically have and need to express more – especially physical –aggression than girls (and women).

However, from the very first stages of our socialization, between the ages of one and three, it is imperative that our instinctual aggression be expressed in ways *other than* 1) harm to ourselves, 2) harm to other people, and 3) harm to other people's property. If parents make clear – which is possible even to a two-year-old – that these things are, and always will be, taboo, they are unlikely to have any serious problems containing the aggression of their children.

Pretend-aggression against other people is common amongst six- to twelve-year-old children, especially boys. I believe it would be unfairly restrictive of children's natural developmental fantasy of being omnipotent controllers of the universe – even to arbitrating life and death – to deny them toy guns and other weaponry, if this is what they most want at this stage.

(See also **Bullying, Fighting, Quarrelling, Timidity.**)

Allergies

Allergic responses – rashes, eczema, hay fever, asthma, etc. – are known to be the body's bid to fight off substances which are toxic to it. However, it is common knowledge, as well as received medical opinion, that psychological stress is an exacerbating, if not a primary, cause.

We are all subject to psychological stresses in our lives, and it seems that some people are just constitutionally predisposed to respond to stress with allergic responses, while others respond with, say, anxiety or irritability.

To the extent that an individual is an 'allergic type', it is my observation that the medicinal treatment of a given allergy may suppress that particular reaction to certain substances, only to be replaced by another allergic response by the body to another substance. For example, a child's 'hives' may disappear when she stops eating strawberries and tomatoes, only to be shortly replaced by a new allergy, say hay fever, in response to cut flowers. So I am inclined to the view that a certain degree of acceptance that a child tends to be an 'allergic type' is appropriate. This can be less exhausting than going to extreme lengths – such as making one's home entirely dust-free! Such extreme efforts are not only often a fruitless waste of energy, but also express a high degree of anxiety on the part of the parent. This is inevitably communicated to the child, and can actually exacerbate the child's allergic responses.

In my opinion, to the extent that allergies represent a combination of bodily and psychological characteristics in a child, the most efficacious treatment is likely to be found through consultation with a homeopathic physician. He or she, by definition, treats the 'whole person' rather than just the bodily symptoms.

(See also **Asthma, Illness, Worrying about your child.**)

Anger

Anger is the expression of righteous outrage in passing judgement of wrong-doing by another person. It is a healthy expression of a developed moral code and should be appreciated as such by parents when displayed by their children. If and when a child expresses genuine anger towards his or her parents, it behoves loving parents to apologize to their children, if appropriate, or respectfully to explain to the child that he or she has misconstrued the meaning of the parent's action.

Inasmuch as anger depends on a developed sense of morality, it is not possible for a child to express genuine anger until near the end of the three- to six-year stage of his or her development. Apparent anger before – and often after! – this time, is most likely to be the expression of the frustration of impulse, which frustration is necessarily often imposed on a child by its parents, especially between the ages of one and three.

(See also **Apologizing, Bullying, Frustration, Timidity.**)

Anorexia Nervosa

Contrary to popular misunderstanding (and to much medical misunderstanding as well!) anorexia nervosa is *not* usually an eating disorder. I believe it to be a complex expression in the child of the consequences of her experience of a profoundly unhealthy *family life*. The child deeply – but largely unconsciously – believes that the welfare of both her parents depends on her continued presence in the family *as a child*. This is usually a partially true psychological perception: typically, the parents often have a loveless marriage, and the father largely absents himself from the family with the self-justification that his wife has the children to keep her happy. The child also experiences incomprehensible hostility expressed by her mother towards her, which she can only make sense of by interpreting it as her just dessert *because she moves and/or because she is visible.*

Her compulsive starvation of herself serves three (incipiently insane) motives. The first is to *stay a child*: the starvation inhibits her physical maturation, and especially menstruation, which is the most overt sign of her outgrowing childhood. The second is to control her body to *stop moving*, even internally: this is manifest, for example, in constipation and the cessation of sweating, common responses of the body to starvation. The third motive is to *become invisible*: this prompts her to perceive herself as 'fat' as long as she can see a 'visible' reflection of herself in the mirror. Thus the real meaning of anorexia nervosa, in terms of the child's actual motivations in starving herself, makes it an extremely serious, life-threatening disease.

The usual necessary condition for a child to develop anorexia, as perceived by most psychotherapists, is that the child's same-sexed parent is 'child-like' – that is tends to present herself to the world as generally helpless and dependent on the care of others – and the child's opposite-sexed parent is 'distant' – that is tends to present himself to the world as overwhelmingly concerned with his work and very little with emotional relationships. Thus because it is more usual in our culture for women to express their neuroses in 'child-like' symptoms and men to express their neuroses in emotional detachment, the disease is overwhelmingly more common in girls than in boys.

It is imperative that the whole family gets competent psychotherapeutic help to ensure the recovery of the child. The first steps are often made by the psychotherapist explaining the psychological meaning of the girl's illness to her father. He or she will enlist the father's active cooperation by asking him to develop and improve the intimacy between himself and his daughter that has been lacking in the past. In particular, an anorexic girl is often greatly facilitated in her recovery by her father's explicit pride in and appreciation of her sexual attractiveness. The relationship between the mother and daughter, however, is usually more difficult to heal because of the mother's typical infantilism. It is often appropriate, therefore, for the psychotherapist to counsel the daughter to use women *other* than her mother as feminine role models. For this reason, a female therapist is usually more suited than a male therapist to the treatment of an anorexic girl.

While the family scenario I have described is by far the most common setting for anorexia nervosa to develop in a child, there are other exceptional conditions that can precipitate the disease. For example, I was recently consulted by a previously healthy thirty-seven-year-old woman who, overnight as it were, became anorexic in response to her husband of fifteen years' standing suddenly leaving her for another woman. The *sexual humiliation* experienced by this woman was more than she could bear, so her unconscious mind – which is much cleverer in all of us than our conscious minds! – came to her rescue by reducing her to a *pre-sexual* state of being through the disease of anorexia. This made her invulnerable to her otherwise unbearable humiliation and loss of self-esteem. (She spontaneously recovered from her anorexia a couple of years later, by which time she had taken appropriate steps to regain her sexual self-esteem sufficiently to bear the reality of what her husband had done to her.)

(See also **Bulimia, Regression.**)

Anxiety

Anxiety is *irrational fear*. When we are rationally afraid, we are responding appropriately to something that actually threatens our well-being. When we are anxious, we are responding as if there were something actually threatening our well-being – when there isn't. In primordial times, when human beings had to fend for themselves in the jungle, most fears were rational. In modern life most of our fears are irrational.

Anxiety in a child (or adult) is best dissolved – or at least diminished – by a light-hearted, but not dismissive approach. For example, 'It's true some dogs do bite, but most of them are very friendly. I'm sure this one is friendly. Look, he's wagging his tail when I stroke him. Go on, you stroke him too.'

(See also **Fear, Magic, Phobias, Worrying about your child.**)

Apologizing

Like real loving, real apologizing is a very grown-up art. Only those who love themselves (through being abundantly and unconditionally loved by their parents) can really love another. Only those who feel themselves to be essentially 'good' (by being made to feel so by their overwhelmingly approving parents) can sometimes authentically admit to being 'bad' or 'wrong', and to apologize for the fact. Getting children mechanically to 'say sorry' achieves nothing positive and may be the basis of a later rebellious resistance to apologizing even when they might otherwise do so.

Apologize freely to your children when you have wronged them, and they will automatically acquire a healthy ability to apologize when they believe they have wronged you or others (but only after they have developed a sense of morality, between the ages of three and six).

(See also **Righteousness.**)

Appetite

See **Eating.**

Asthma

Asthma is a common allergic condition which is normally outgrown by puberty. Symptomatically, it can be very frightening to both the child and its parents although, as far as possible, parents should hide their own anxiety from the child, which otherwise exacerbates the child's anxiety and, in turn, exacerbates his or her asthma.

There is general agreement amongst physicians and psychotherapists that *suppressed aggression*, as well as physical allergy, is often an important component causative agent in asthma. To this extent, some vigorous sport, especially one involving running, often facilitates cure, although parents need the assurance of their physician that this is a safe remedial activity for their child.

(See also **Aggression, Allergies, Anxiety, Illness, Worrying about your child.**)

Attachments

We all begin life completely self-centred, with no concern for anybody but ourselves. Only very gradually do we become capable of showing loving concern for other people. 'Attachments' – to our own thumb, a specially loved stuffed toy, a dirty old piece of cloth, etc. – represent a transitional stage between total self-centredness and love for other people. Usually, by about the age of six, most 'transitional objects' have been abandoned in favour of emotional attachments to real people. However, there are residual manifestations of every stage of our development in all of us, and even some fully 'grown-up' people remain attached to some special object from which they gain comfort or reassurance when the going gets rough in their relationships.

Respect the objects to which your child is especially attached, and make sure they are available to her when she is unavoidably stressed.

(See also **Companions, Magic, Pets, Regression.**)

Autism

Autism is an extremely pathological psychological condition, usually diagnosable between the ages of about one to three, the core symptom being the child's *inability to make emotional contact with any other human being*. It goes without saying that this is profoundly distressing to loving parents.

The causes of autism are far from fully understood, although the evidence to date suggests it is probably produced by a combination of an innate predisposition and some localized, specific brain damage, probably occurring in the course of a difficult (usually first) labour in the mother, perhaps associated with the administration of oxygen to the baby in the process of its birth.

While the general prognosis for autism is poor, not all cases are equally severe. Approximately half of all autistic children do have some speech and, amongst these, a considerable degree of cure can be achieved through 'behaviour modification' therapy.

Baby-talk

While baby-talk to a baby is instinctive and right and good, once a child is about twelve months old and beginning spontaneously to utter real words, baby-talk by parents to the child should be avoided. Baby-talk patronizes a child, and the child knows it and doesn't like it. I recall reading a book about the development of language in children in which the following story was told. A father came home from work and went into the bathroom to say hello to his two-year-old son who was having a bath. The father said, 'What are you doing?' His son replied, 'I'm playing with my fis.' Father said, 'Oh, you're playing with your fis, are you?' 'No, my *fis*.' 'Oh, your *fish*?' 'Yes, my fis.'

However, I personally dislike the super-adult, clinical approach of some parents, who insist, for example, on 'penis' and 'umbilicus' rather than 'willie' and 'belly button'. In this I may be expressing no more than my own preference, but my rationalization of my preference is that it is wholly natural for young children (especially between the ages of three and six) to find their own and other people's genitals, other 'private parts' and excreta extremely mirthful, and I think they should have 'funny' names to match.

(See also **Regression.**)

Bathing

Contemporary increasing awareness of the widespread existence of child sexual abuse prompts many wholly innocent parents to wonder if they may be inadvertently so abusing their children. Generally speaking, it is only in bathing children that parents touch their children's genitals. In this context I would recommend that a child over the age of four not be bathed by his or her opposite-sexed parent, and that the child be encouraged from about this age to wash his or her own genitals.

(See also **Child abuse, Three to six.**)

Bed-wetting

After the age of about four, bed-wetting is almost always an expression of nervousness in the child, representing some psychological dis-ease. While I hope it goes without saying that no reader of this book would punish a child for bed-wetting, it is also important to realize that a parent's own anxiety about the issue will be picked up by the child, add to his nervousness, and perpetuate the problem. The best approach is to discover, subtly, without directly confronting the child, if there is anything that is worrying him and to eliminate that worry, when the bed-wetting will cease. In the mean time, the best immediate response to the wet bed is a matter-of-fact, 'Oh dear, you had an accident. Never mind.'

If the symptom is long-lasting, consult your physician to check there is no physical cause. If, thereafter, the symptom continues inexplicably, consult a child psychotherapist to uncover the underlying dis-ease in the child.

(See also **Nervousness.**)

Birth order

The contingent fact, for each of us, of being the eldest, youngest, in the middle, or an only child within our family has a marked effect on our personalities for the whole of our lives. Parenthood is always a tightrope act, in which each child, at every stage of his or her development, needs to be encouraged to stretch his present abilities forward into the next stage of his development, while at the same time being permitted to remain in his present stage of development – and even, in response to stress, temporarily to regress to an earlier stage of development – until his present competences are fully consolidated. Needless to say, it is impossible for parents always to get this balancing act 'just right', so the result for everybody is that we each tend to be predisposed to an imbalance in our personalities (throughout our lives) between being too grown-up and responsible (to the detriment of our needs to play and express dependency) and being too childlike and dependent (to the detriment of our self-sufficiency and autonomy).

The personalities of oldest children are almost always over-emphatically responsible and sensible; of youngest children over-emphatically dependent and compliant. Only children tend to acquire personalities that contain elements of both too great self-sufficiency *and* too great compliant dependency. In families of three children, the first child often welcomes the birth of the third child as an ally against the second child of whom he is typically very jealous, and, over the years, the second child may easily be made, by the first child's manipulation, to have a personality that proclaims, 'I am the odd one out.'

While it is unrealistic and unnecessary for parents to demand of themselves that they create 'perfectly balanced' children, it makes sense, once in a while, purposefully to redress the imbalances created by birth order. They could, for example, play 'irresponsibly' with an oldest child (while his or her younger siblings are out of the way), or demand singular responsibility of a youngest child (even while his or her older siblings are around).

(See also **Only child, Permissions, Regression, Spacing of children.**)

Birth story

A remarkable fact that I have discovered in my practice as a psychotherapist is that what we each remember being told about our birth is a precise metaphor for the way we relate in general to all other people. What we remember is not always what we were actually told: that is, we at least partly (and unconsciously) *create* 'the story of our birth' in our minds as a fitting metaphor for the way we actually relate to other people. However, it requires a bit of an imaginative leap to translate the literal statement about your birth into the psychological statement about the way you tend to relate to other people. Thus an adult who – for whatever reasons – is lacking in understanding of the basis of his or her choice of friends and acquaintances and how he or she relates to them, will say, in response to the question, 'What do you know about your birth?' 'I don't know anything about my birth.' A woman who consulted me told me, 'When my mother was pregnant with me, nearly all foods made her feel very sick. But there were a few foods she really loved and ate all the time.' I translated this to mean that this woman doesn't like most people, but she has a few friends who are very dear to her. I asked her if this was so and, with amazement, she affirmed it was. And a paranoid schizophrenic who once consulted me, replied to the question, 'When I was born they held me upside down, and I cried and they laughed.'

So, while the actual facts of our birth, as told to us by our parents, cannot be said to be deterministic causes of the ways in which we relate to other people, it is obviously a good idea for parents to encourage their children, volitionally, to have the most positive possible 'birth story'. 'I had a terrible time', if accepted by the child as the foundation of the birth story he creates in his mind, will have the effect of making all his relationships very painful; 'I nearly died' will make him perceive himself as 'nearly destroying' the people he relates to; and 'You nearly died' will make him experience himself as 'nearly destroyed' by other people in his relationships with them. As a safe bet, a mother should say (as many do), 'It was the most wonderful experience of my life, and everybody was very happy.'

Blaming

See **Righteousness.**

Bravery

There is a fine line between the virtue of bravery in the face of un-avoidable pain – physical or moral – and its 'inhuman' excess which manifests as cold, stiff-upper-lipped suppression of emotional responsiveness (traditionally so prized by British public schools). As in so many aspects of child-rearing, the encouragement of the virtue of bravery within appropriate limits is a tightrope act that loving parents are required to perform.

(See also **Comforting, Illness, Protectiveness.**)

Bribery

Do not be diffident about bribing your child in circumstances where you want him or her to do something out of the ordinary that he or she is resistant to doing. 'Bribery' sounds bad, but it is actually another word for negotiation: it effectively says, 'I'll do this for you if you do this for me', which is the underlying – although often heavily camouflaged – basis of all human interaction. However, to the extent that bribery usually implies the offering of a *material* reward, it should be reserved for special occasions to avoid spoiling the child. In all ordinary circumstances, the child should be expected to be implicitly obedient to the general rules of life as laid down by the parents from their rightful authority.

Bribery is especially useful in instances where a parent is somewhat doubtful of the meaning of the child's resistance to doing something, and the parent wants to avoid brutally over-riding the child's possible fear. So, for example, a child's tearful clinging to his mother on his first two or three days at nursery school is almost certainly the expression of his fear of separation from his mother, and it is most appropriate for his mother to stay with him for a while and gradually ease him into allowing her to leave him there. If his tearful clinging is undiminished after a few days, it may be that he is no longer really frightened, but is manipulatively exploiting his mother's anxiety on his behalf. This is a good time to bribe him with a new toy he particularly desires, promised to him for 'when you stay at nursery school without Mummy and you don't cry'. If, despite his desire for the wanted toy, he still cries and clings to his mother, he is not yet ready to be left. If he stays without her and without crying, he is ready to be left – and should, of course, be given the promised toy promptly. Any crying and clinging on subsequent days should, at least in the first instance, be presumed to be a manipulative ploy to extract another bribe from his mother – which should be firmly resisted!

(See also **Control, Discipline, Obedience, Punishment, Spoiling.**)

Bulimia

Bulimia describes the condition of a child who compulsively and literally stuffs herself full of food and then disgorges herself by vomiting or purging. Notwithstanding that it is symptomatically the opposite of anorexia nervosa (in which the child compulsively starves herself), it is actually a manifestation of the same underlying, extremely serious *psychological* dis-ease. In some cases, compulsive starving alternates with compulsive gorging, although others display only one of these symptoms. Physically, bulimia is as life-threatening as anorexia. It leads to severe pathology of the digestive tract and may eventually result in death through sudden rupturing of the stomach.

(See also **Anorexia nervosa**.)

Bullying

A bully is likely to be a child who, in bullying weaker or easily frightened other children, is behaving as his physically and/or psychologically abusive father (or mother) does towards him. The bully is almost certainly a very unhappy and frightened child who is already profoundly committed to an angry, bitter, defeatist attitude to life.

Ironically, the bully's chosen victim may very well be a child who has been similarly abused in his family, but who succumbs to his defeatism wholeheartedly rather than via the detour of compensatory aggression. Just as often, though, the victim is a child who is tenderly loved and feels uncomprehendingly overwhelmed by the bully's tactics. In these cases the bully is – consciously or unconsciously – acting out his rageful envy against children who are clearly so much more loved than he is.

If possible, it is preferable to teach the victim how *not* to collude with the bully, rather than rescuing him with the power of your own intervention. The victim's fear can be largely dissipated by explaining to him – in words appropriate to his understanding – that the bully is actually a very frightened child himself.

Should your own child show signs of being a bully, he is almost certainly signalling his present very low self-esteem. This, in a usually loved and loving child, is probably a response to some present trauma in his life, such as his parents' divorce. Read his signal as the bid for reassurance and love that it is, rather than criticizing or otherwise punishing him, which will only exacerbate the problem by lowering his self-esteem even more.

(See also **Aggression, Child Abuse, Timidity**.)

Character

Character – contrasted with personality or temperament, which is largely innate – is wholly formed by instruction. It refers to firmly entrenched beliefs about what is moral and 'good' and what is immoral and 'bad', which beliefs and values direct us in *nurturing and controlling* ourselves as well as others.

We are 'wired' to be most receptive to moral exhortation from three to six and subsidiarily in adolescence. Children who are not explicitly taught a moral code by the exhortations of their parents (supported by their other teachers, who represent the culture's values) between three and six years of age will find it very difficult to make up for this lack later on, and are likely always to have *weak characters* – that is, they will have a poorly developed sense of right and wrong and, in extreme cases, will be lawless psychopaths. Children internalize the values given them by their parents and have them for life (even though you wouldn't think so at puberty and even maybe up until their mid-twenties!).

(See also **Conscience, Guilt, Morality.**)

Child abuse

Child abuse encapsulates the timeless truth that 'the sins of the fathers are visited upon the children even unto the third and fourth generation'. Properly loved children grow up to be loving people in general and loving parents in particular; abused children grow up to be unloving people in general and abusing parents in particular.

Child abuse is the evil inflicted by the powerful on the powerless in the interest of the powerful perpetrator defending his or her own sick self. Abuse may take the form of physical or psychological brutality towards the child, or sexual interference with the child. The damage to the child's well-being is likely to be lifelong.

It is my belief that the only way society has open to it effectively to break into the self-perpetuating horror of child abuse is by teaching our children, from five years old onwards, about the psychology of human relationships. When psychological literacy is as valued and as mandatory as basic literacy and numeracy in our educational system, we may find that we have produced an 'inoculation' against child abuse that wipes it out as effectively as we have wiped out polio and smallpox.

(See also **Aggression, Bathing, Bullying, Fear, Good and Evil, Love, Smacking.**)

Child care

Parenthood, especially motherhood, and especially in the pre-school years, is the most demanding and exhausting job on earth. Whether or not a mother is bound by material necessity to leave her young child in order to earn money, there are times when she is bound to want – and be entitled to – some regular, short breaks from her child to maintain her own sense of well-being and selfhood.

For a child under the age of about two, do your best to leave her only with her father or some other relative who deeply loves her, such as grandma. When these options are not available, if at all possible, limit yourself to one carer only, whose visits the child experiences utterly predictably and reliably.

Between about two and three a child begins to be capable of enjoying a couple of hours at a time playing alongside other children she knows, in the care of their mothers but in the absence of her own. So, from this age onwards, 'baby-sitting pools' can be a cost-free boon to mothers, who inevitably and rightfully long for just a little time to read a book, paint a picture, buy a dress, have a bath . . .or just stare into space, in peace!

From the age of three onwards a child is becoming a truly social being and, for her healthy development, needs regular times away from her mother every bit as much as her mother needs times away from her. Four or five half-days a week at nursery school provide the ideal fulfilment of a three to five year old's and her mother's needs for separation from each other.

(See also **Separation, Working mothers.**)

Choices

Do not, in the name of kindness, make the mistake of driving a child to paralyzed confusion or hysteria by giving her more choices than she is capable of making. We all want to have our cake and eat it. It is hard enough fo grown-ups to accept that this cannot be, and it is cruelly nerve-wracking to children to underline this dilemma in them by giving them more than a minimum of either/or choices. As a rule of thumb, it is probably kindest to offer a child under about two and a half *no choices* (especially in matters of food) and, for even several years thereafter, only 'vanilla or chocolate?' rather than 'vanilla or chocolate or strawberry?'.

Clingingness

Clingingness is a manifestation of a child's awareness of how much he depends on his mother's loving presence for his survival, and usually begins at about seven or eight months. (Before this time, the infant is blissfully ignorant of the specificity of his dependence on his mother, even though her presence pleases him more than any other.) It continues, diminishingly, until about three (with escalations at times of significant stress).

The clingingness of a child is nerve-wrackingly irritating to most mothers. However, it needs to be understood as a natural and necessary manifestation of the child's transitional ambivalence concerning being wholly and safely attached to his mother, and venturing forth into the exciting, but comparatively unsafe, world away from her.

Any but sporadic clingingness over the age of three suggests that either the child is experiencing some basic insecurity – in which case the insecurity rather than the symptom of clingingness needs to be understood and overcome – or that his mother, out of her own anxiety, is covertly inviting the child to exploit her. Bribery is usually a good test of whether a child's clingingness expresses a genuine need or is exploitative.

(See also **Anxiety, Bribery, Dependency, Insecurity, Regression, Safety, Separation, Whining, Worrying about your child.**)

Comforting

When a child is hurt – physically or emotionally – he deserves loving comforting. However, bear in mind that all attention (loving or punitive) reinforces the behaviour it is given for. Beware of prolonged comforting of a child, which can lead to the child actually seeking (however unconsciously) painful experiences for himself, in order to receive the comforting he knows he will then get. So, in a general way, make sure you give your child *more* loving attention when he is *not* hurt than when he is.

(See also **Attachments, Bravery, Illness, Protectiveness.**)

Companions

Before the age of about three, children are not emotionally competent to interact with each other as equals in mutually caring and sharing ways. At best, they play warily alongside each other, at worst with unbridled aggressive hostility towards each other.

Between the ages of about eighteen months and three a child is gradually making the transition from being wholly narcissistically self-centred to becoming capable of expressing real (not only 'cupboard') love for others. It is commonplace and healthy at this stage for children to invent imaginary companions whom they talk to and about in anticipatory practice for real friendships that they will begin to form from three onwards.

Don't deny your child this natural expression of her fantasy. You might sometimes enjoy participating in your child's conversation with her imaginary companions, unless, of course, your child makes clear you are not invited to the party.

(See also **Attachments, Fantasy, Friends, Loneliness, Sociability.**)

Competitiveness

Competitiveness in all human beings is a manifestation of the desire to feel superior to other people as a compensation for an underlying feeling of inferiority. In an ideal world, the self-esteem of all grown-ups would be so well-established that they would all realize they were 'above average' in a few matters, 'below average' in a few matters, and essentially the *equal* of all other human beings (in a hundred years we'll all be dust!) and competitiveness would be redundant.

However, competitiveness is a natural part of child development because the essential truth of the matter for children is that they *are* inferior to grown-ups in their inability to look after themselves and be self-sufficient, of which fact they are poignantly aware. So their need to develop their self-esteem is served by competitiveness.

Competitiveness increases as children grow up, and the closer they get to self-sufficiency the more aware they are of their residual 'inferiority' to grown-ups. Their frustration and anger at their dependency, and their associated response of competitiveness reaches its peak in adolescence (which follows the twelve- to sixteen-year-old stage of their development during which they seek to evade the issue by grandiosity), the final issue being the matter of their sexual potency and attractiveness. Their same-sexed parent is seen as their chief rival, and it behoves parents, at this stage, explicitly but subtly to make the child feel 'superior' to them, by giving the child a great deal of praise, and underplaying their own self-esteem. For example, it does a teenage boy a power of good to win a race against his father; and it does a teenage girl a power of good to hear her mother remark that she is getting grey and wrinkly!

The school system implicitly and positively exploits the competitiveness of adolescents with competitive sports and with examinations, the passing of which does much to consolidate a child's achievement of 'grown-up' self-esteem.

(See also **Envy, Jealousy, Rivalry.**)

Compulsions

Compulsions are ritualistic patterns of thought or behaviour performed over and over again by a child – or grown-up – in a superstitious bid to ward off some presumed harm she will suffer if she desists. Traced to its limit, the 'harm' the child (or adult) fears is death, and the compulsion is a – conscious or unconscious – bid to defy death with magic. Compulsions are especially common in children between the ages of six and twelve, at which time a child begins realistically to know that she and the people she loves are mortal, and that death is irreversible.

I remember dealing effectively with one of my daughter's compulsions when she was about ten by exploiting the 'magic' involved, with my own 'greater magic'. She had started compulsively touching doorknobs a certain number of times every time she entered or left a room. I noticed that the number of times she bound herself to touch the doorknobs was steadily increasing and beginning seriously to interfere with her everyday life, as, for instance, in so delaying her that she would miss her bus to school. So I decided that some intervention was called for, and one night as she was going to bed I said, casually (so as not to shame her), 'You know how you keep touching doorknobs?' 'Yes.' 'Do you do it to stop something horrible happening?' Tentatively, 'Yes.' 'Well,' I said, 'I'll tell you why you have to do it. It's because a wicked witch cast a spell on you; but I can undo it, because mothers' spells are more powerful than witches'. When I say "Abracadabra" three times you'll never have to touch doorknobs again, and nothing bad will happen to you.' It worked – like a charm!

(It might be objected that a ten-year-old child would know that spells were 'not true' and so she would not be susceptible to them. This was so, but only as far as her rational, conscious mind was concerned. Her equally powerful *irrational* mind knew differently, and happily responded to the magic.)

(See also **Death, Good and Evil, Habits, Magic, Six to twelve.**)

Conformity

A certain degree of conformity is essential to our survival and our social acceptability. We are 'wired' to be most receptive to demands made on us to conform between about one and three years of age. At this time parents accept their responsibility to *impose* on their child good manners and other 'conformities' such as *not* running on to the road and *not* poking screwdrivers into electric sockets. These controls need to be autocratically given to serve the combined interests of the preservation of the child's life and his socialization, long before he has the character or the reasoning ability judiciously to decide these things for himself.

All conformity imposed on a child (especially between the ages of one and three) is internalized by the child with very great power and *for the rest of his life*, irrespective of the objective value it has for him. So (especially when a child is one to three years old), it behoves loving parents scrupulously to resist demanding conformity of their child beyond that which is strictly necessary for his survival and his basic social acceptability. This because all conformity is, by definition, a denial of some aspect of the spontaneous and joyful expressiveness of impulse and emotion with which we are born and which so enhances the whole of our lives.

At puberty and into adolescence *anti*-conformity is a natural form of conformity. That is, in separating from parents, a child inevitably goes through a stage of finding security in conformity with his peers, but against his parents. At the same time he is also confusedly ashamed of his parents for any perception he has of *their* non-conformity.

(See also **Defiance, Obedience, One to three, Reasoning, Rebellion, Sociability.**)

Conscience

Our conscience consists of the areas of our minds that prompt us to behave morally rather than immorally, even when nobody is looking and we know we could not be found out. If we disobey our conscience we punish ourselves with guilt, which hurts us as much as the wrath of our parents did when they first taught us the difference between 'right' and 'wrong'. By and large our conscience is our parents' morality incorporated into our own minds.

When a child is between three and six and at the peak of acquiring her conscience, she may become temporarily excessively *self*-punitive for the most venial wrong she considers herself to have committed. Parents need to mitigate such excess with appropriate reassurance, such as, 'Never mind. It was an accident. I'm not cross. I know you didn't mean to break it.'

(See also **Accidents, Guilt, Morality.**)

Constipation

In the absence of any physical pathology, constipation is often a sign that there is an unhealthy power struggle occurring between the child and one or other of his parents. A child's ability to control his bowel movements is symbolically, for the child, a proud achievement of his *autonomy*, and the pleasure he gives his mother (or father) in 'having a poo poo' appropriately, on the toilet, is the first 'gift' he is able to give.

Psychologically-induced constipation in a child is a defensive response of stubbornness against a parent's bid to *over-control* the child concerning the way he behaves in general and/or his bowel movements in particular. However, parents who over-control their children are likely themselves to be over-controlled, and are naturally, therefore, inclined to justify their over-control of their children as right and proper. So I can only suggest that parents of a constipated child honestly reflect on the possibility that *they* were over-controlled children, and that they would like to give their own children the benefit of an easier, free-er upbringing.

(See also **Control, Independence, Obedience, Potty Training, Rebellion.**)

Control

Being in control of a child (which often takes effort and perseverance) is an intrinsic part of loving a child – and the child knows it. It is *not* loving to give in to a child's persistent demands on a matter 'for the sake of peace', when your better judgement says 'no'. Children know, in a vague way, that the outcome of fulfilling their every immediate desire is not always happy. They rely on the greater knowledge and conviction of their parents to stop them doing what, on balance, would not be good for them, even though they, the children, are bound to cause a fuss at the time. *Appropriately controlled children feel loved, uncontrolled children feel unloved.*

Where possible, give a simple reason for your prohibition – 'You can't have another biscuit now because you've had two already and, if you have another one, you'll get tummy-ache.' Sometimes, though, the reason for your prohibition is beyond the comprehension of the child and you simply have to assert the authority of your greater wisdom. For example, to a fifteen-year-old who moans and groans that physics is 'too difficult' and 'irrelevant' and he wants to 'drop it', a loving parent does *not* usually say, 'Well, if it really is hard for you, give it up', but rather, 'Everything worth doing is hard. I know better than you do now that getting your GCSE physics will be very worthwhile for you, and I know you are perfectly capable of doing it. Now get on with your homework, and don't let me hear any more nonsense about it!'

By means of such controlling responses, not only is a child's character developed, but your exhortation to him or her simply to 'get on with it' powerfully implies your greater belief in his ability than he presently has. You are contributing thereby to the growth of his self-esteem. 'Letting a child off' anything that he claims is 'too difficult' reinforces his low self-esteem that has prompted his desire to 'cop out'. While it is, of course, also demeaning of a child's self-esteem to demand more than he is capable of, when in doubt, impose on him the burden of your expectation of his success rather than the humiliation of your assessment of him being no higher than his own (presently low) self-esteem.

(See also **Constipation, Discipline, Firmness, Flexibility, Frustration, Obedience, Permissiveness, Prohibitions, Punishment.**)

Criticism

I firmly believe that *all criticism of one human being by another is destructive*, that is, that there is no such thing as 'constructive criticism'. This does not mean that a child (or adult) never deserves *correction* – which is quite a different thing. There is all the difference in the world between, for example, 'The trouble with you is you are mean' and 'That was a mean thing to do.' The former implies an unchanging attribute of the accused, which powerfully influences him or her to diminished self-esteem. The latter implies that the accused chose to behave in an undesirable way – and *behaviour is of this moment only* and may be freely changed by anybody at their will.

It is hard enough for grown-ups to disbelieve critical attributions imposed on them. For children, criticism is agonizing because they deeply believe everything they are told about themselves (especially by their parents), and the critical attributions imposed on them are likely to be painful negative beliefs they hold about themselves for the rest of their lives. A great deal of the work done by psychotherapists is struggling to get their (grown-up) patients to disavow the negative attributions imposed on them by their parents which have caused them continuing unhappiness in their lives.

(See also **Punishment.**)

Crying

By and large a baby's crying means she is in pain or otherwise distressed, and a parent's instinctive and healthy response is to rush to stop the cause and, so, the crying. However, it is also important to remember that crying is the only language a baby has, and sometimes does not need intervention. Most parents learn quite quickly to differentiate various tones of crying in their baby, and it is particularly valuable to distinguish the one that just means, 'I'm so tired, I'll lull myself to sleep with the sound of my own voice.' Overanxious parents of a new baby often *cause* distress in him by picking him up to soothe such crying, rather than allowing him to sing himself to sleep.

Crying in older children (and adults) is more singularly associated with an overflow of unhappy feelings, which should, of course, be allowed. But ignore the attempted blackmail of a child who seeks to exploit you through crying as a means of pulling at your heartstrings and so getting from you what you would otherwise not be willing to grant.

Curiosity

Curiosity is the mental aliveness in us all. How wonderful it would be if we could maintain all our lives the curiosity of a young child in response to the exciting newness she finds in the world and life itself. Notwithstanding the exhaustion imposed on parents by the necessity to constrain their young child physically from hurting herself, other people, or other people's property, and answering her continuous barrage of 'why', 'how', 'what', 'when','where', do your best to relish and endorse her curiosity about anything and everything. And do let her stare!

(See also **Learning, One to three, Six months to one year.**)

Custody

But for exceptional cases, when children can live with only one of their parents, their mother is the one who can nourish them best. However, the profoundly influential and lifelong consequences of the Oedipus complex in all our lives determines that at the critical ages of three to six and adolescence it is extremely unhealthy for a child to be in the sole custody of his or her opposite-sexed parent.

In adolescence, if at all possible, a son whose parents live separately should complete his emotional-sexual maturation by spending some years living with his father; and a daughter with her mother. By this means the child is given the opportunity to form a sound gender identity through association with his or her same-sexed parent, and to avoid the deeply damaging consequences of 'possessing' his or her opposite-sexed parent.

I recall a man of twenty-eight who consulted me because he found himself repeatedly in 'suffocating' relationships with women whom he didn't really like because he compulsively (but unconsciously) attracted clingingly dependent women and passively allowed himself to be drawn into intimacy with them. He was an only child whose father died when he was fourteen. He remembers that his first thought when he heard his father had died was, 'Ha ha, now I've got her [his mother] all to myself.' For this illegitimate victory, his unconscious punished him with the pain of being 'bound' to her forever – even though he defended himself against realizing this by 'proving' how successfully he was separated from his mother by the outward show of his multitude of girlfriends (who were all, in fact, his mother in disguise).

(See also **Adolescence, Divorce, Sexuality, Three to six.**)

Death

A fully realistic understanding of death develops in a child between the ages of six and twelve. He now knows its irreversibility and the fact that everybody, including himself, must one day die. He explicitly fears his own death and the deaths of his parents (on whom he feels he depends for his own survival).

In grown-ups who feel they have lived and are living their lives to the full, the fear of death gradually diminishes as their dreams of the potential future for themselves are actualized. In children, all of their ambitions for themselves are unrealized, and so their fear of death – however unspoken – is very great.

The fear of death is defended against by all human beings – and exaggeratedly so in six- to twelve-year-old children – in ritual, magical incantations, and diverse forms of obsessive-compulsive behaviour, by which means we seek to 'stop bad things happening', the ultimate 'bad thing' being death. However unspoken a child's fear of death is, parents need to be sensitive to it. If a child does express explicit fear of his own or others' deaths, in normal circumstances, he should be told something along the lines of, 'Yes, everybody dies one day, but not until they are ready. Mummy and Daddy and you probably won't die for a very, very, very long time, until we've done all the things we want to.' Do *not* describe death as 'like going to sleep', which readily invokes in a child a fear of going to sleep; nor even 'stopping breathing', which may prompt a child to fear that unless he self-consciously breathes he will die. Probably the best verbalization for a child is some form of tautology like, 'You just stop being alive.'

When a grandparent or other loved old person dies, a child might be told, 'She was happy to die, because she'd had her turn of being alive and had done all the things she wanted to do. Of course it's sad for us that we won't see her again, but she can still make us happy when we remember her and talk about her.'

When the death of a loved relative or friend is tragically untimely, there is an added dimension of anger and (irrational) guilt that needs to be expressed by the bereaved survivors. The death of either parent before a child has reached full maturity – which is actually as late as about thirty years of age – is probably the greatest tragedy that can befall a child. At the deepest level of the child's being, the untimely death of a parent is experienced as overwhelming abandonment and cannot but have profound and permanent psychological consequences for the child. A secondary consequence of the premature death of a parent – especially a child's same-sexed parent – is the child's appreciation of the 'unfairness' of the fact that his parent was not granted enough life to fulfil his or her potential. This fact may seriously inhibit the child in fulfilling his own potential throughout his life. That is, it is as if the child is unwilling to exploit his 'unfair advantage' of more life to live than his parent had. The negativity of these consequences can be minimized by the prompt help of a competent psychotherapist, who can facilitate the child in 'working through' the implications of his bereavement before they are unhealthily suppressed or repressed.

(See also **Abandonment, Compulsions, God, Grief, Magic.**)

Defiance

As grown-ups we appreciate that it is usually appropriate to comply with the demands of rightful authorities, but also appropriate sometimes to defy authorities we believe to be unjust. Parents are children's primary 'authority', and it is in relation to their parents that children learn healthily to respect authority, while at the same time leaving some space in their minds for occasional stand-up-and-be-counted defiance. Thus children are bound to say 'no' as well as 'yes' to their parents, in order to develop individualistic spiritedness as well as 'niceness' in relation to other people and the world.

Parents need to walk the tightrope of expecting and demanding general obedience from their children, while giving them a little scope for some undisciplined defiance. Many acts of defiance contain their own punishment, anyhow, such as breaking a toy that is not handled with appropriate care, or feeling tired and miserable the next day after refusing to have enough sleep. Avoid saying, 'I told you so' after the event. The child knows you did, and reminding him of the fact unnecessarily rubs salt into the wound.

'No!' is particularly rife at two and a half, and again at puberty. (See also **Conformity, Disobedience, Obedience, Rebellion.**)

Delinquency

Delinquency is an assumed amoral attitude, and a commonplace symptom of the natural and healthy rebelliousness of puberty. Often, in an act of delinquency, a child is – largely unconsciously – testing the stringency of the morality of his parents, and is grateful for their serious concern and outrage in response to his delinquent act. This is usually all that is needed for him never to do such a thing again.

Delinquent behaviour before or after puberty is a sign that the child is seriously emotionally and/or morally disturbed and is in need of psychotherapeutic help.

(See also **Control, Morality, Stealing, Thirteen to sixteen.**)

Dependency

There are few species that are as utterly dependent on their parents at birth as a human baby. And it takes longer for a human being to achieve full independent maturity than any other species. The ultimate, biologically informed goal of parenthood is to make our children so thoroughly independent of us that they are not handicapped in their effective functioning by separation from us, nor profoundly traumatized by our timely deaths.

While it is happy and healthy for both parties if and when a grown-up child turns to his or her parents for occasional specific advice or material benefit, at such times parents should remain wary of endorsing or encouraging their child's *neediness* of them. A good sign that a child is achieving healthy independence of his parents is his willingness and ability to stop living with his parents. Probably by the time he is twenty – and certainly by the time he is twenty-five – a healthy child will no longer be living with his parents. He will also be earning his own living, and will feel and be responsible for any debts he incurs.

(See also **Abandonment, Clingingness, Handicaps, Insecurity, Leaving home, Over-protectiveness, Worrying about your child.**)

Depression

At core, depression is a feeling of unworthiness of being loved and essential worthlessness of one's self. It is an aching void that should, healthily, be filled with a feeling of being loved and valued and needed by others for one's own intrinsic worth. It is often associated with the death of a much-loved other person, and may also be associated with the fear of one's own death.

Children are as capable of being depressed as grown-ups, but are not articulate enough to describe the state as grown-ups do. Prolonged quiet withdrawal from activities or from interactions with other people suggests a child may be depressed and in need of being *loved back to life* with abundant physical and verbal expressions of affection. When there is no obvious precipitating cause for a child's depression (such as the death of a loved person or a pet), or justified depression extends into weeks or months, psychotherapeutic help should be sought.

(See also **Abandonment, Grief, Separation, Six to twelve.**)

Discipline

Wholesome disciplining of a child is the obverse of bribery. Both are forms of tit-for-tat. Bribery effectively says, 'You do this nice thing for me and I'll do that nice thing for you'; discipline effectively says, 'You did that nasty thing to me, so I'll do this (similar) nasty thing to you.' The key to disciplining a child wholesomely rather than cruelly, lies in the retribution being comparable to (and maybe less, but never more than) the crime committed. If a child pinches you or kicks you, pinch or kick him back; if a child insistently plays with a fragile object of yours, after you have told him not to, and he breaks it, express your vengeful anger by grabbing his teddy bear by the feet and bashing its head on the ground. Momentarily, the child will be very upset indeed by your 'eye for an eye' retribution, but he will also thereby fully understand the meaning of your anger and the true meaning of justice.

A smack or some other form of punishment by which you express your superior power over the child may be more expedient and less immediately upsetting to the child but, in the long run, he gains nothing from such acts but a lifelong predisposition to feel resentful anger towards all the people he encounters who have some authority over him.

(See also **Bribery, Control, Prohibitions, Punishment, Smacking.**)

Disobedience

A child's disobedience is the natural way in which she tests her parents' power over her. In the early years of childhood a parent is capable, if necessary, of physically preventing his child's disobedience; but increasingly he has to rely on the child's own morality – which he has taught her – to constrain her from behaviour of which he would disapprove.

At puberty and in adolescence a child is likely to *threaten* to disobey her parents much more often than she actually does. She gleefully relishes the anxiety she thus invokes in her parents, and their essential impotence to stop her. But notwithstanding that a twelve- to sixteen-year-old child appears to have cast off altogether the 'shackles' of her upbringing, she hasn't really. She wants you to be appropriately horrified by her threats of amorality, and for you to express the stalwartness of your own values. By this means she is helped to keep herself in check – even though she will never admit this to you!

(See also **Conformity, Conscience, Control, Defiance, Morality, Obedience, Rebellion.**)

Divorce

When parents get divorced a child is deeply disturbed by two inferences he or she makes in response. These inferences may not be uttered aloud by the child but only expressed indirectly in his or her obviously disturbed or regressive behaviour. The two inferences are: 'Mummy and Daddy have got divorced because of me. I did something bad that made them stop loving each other.' And, 'Daddy doesn't love Mummy or me any more, so he has gone away and left us. Perhaps Mummy will stop loving me and she'll go away and leave me.' At the deepest level of their being children of all ages have these thoughts in response to their parents' divorce, but especially so if the divorce occurs when the child is between about three and six or twelve and eighteen years of age. (Contrary to popular belief, a child's capacity to withstand emotional traumas does not increase linearly with age: a child is most vulnerable between the ages of three and six and about thirteen and eighteen, and least vulnerable between the ages of about six and twelve.)

These thoughts in the child need to be countered by both parents explicitly verbalizing many times that the unhappiness between the parents leading to their separation is entirely between them and has *nothing whatsoever to do with the child*. It has to be explained that sometimes mothers and fathers stop loving each other, which is possible between people who are not related to each other, but *mothers and fathers never, never stop loving their children*. Do not be put off repeating these truths to a child many many times in the weeks and months following the divorce, even though the child is likely to respond, after the first couple of times, 'Yeah, yeah. I know.' However dismissive an act the child puts on, he is, in fact, deeply grateful for your reiteration of these truths, which he needs to hear many times to be fully convinced of them.

Some well-meaning parents, when they divorce, tell their children that they, the parents, still like each other and will always be very good friends. This notion is actually very damaging to the child because it creates in his mind an incongruity between the profound unhappiness the break-up of the family causes him and the apparent *insignificance* of the reasons for it. This can devastate his belief in the meaning and significance of love and even of life itself. His psychological well-being is much better served by being told that 'Mummy and Daddy both love you very very much, and we both want to be with you all the time, so we have tried very hard to get on with each other. But we have got to the stage where we make each other so unhappy that we can't bear living with each other any more. So please forgive us for doing this to you.'

The child will forgive you and will probably, in due course, also thank you for relieving him of the hell of living with unhappy parents. Furthermore, your implicit claim to *your* happiness provides him with deep permission to seek his own happiness in life, which is the greatest gift you can bestow on a child. The obverse, of sacrificing your own happiness 'for your child's sake', is one of the cruellest burdens of obligations and guilt that can be imposed on a child.

(See also **Custody, Happiness, Sexuality.**)

Drug abuse

Children are most vulnerable to experimenting with drugs at puberty and in adolescence, and I think the promised euphoria in the face of the huge mood swings they experience in association with their unstable hormonal levels is a more likely cause than simple defiance of their parents' exhortations and controls. The normal rebelliousness of puberty, combined with a premature desire to be fully grown-up and autonomous is certainly likely to find some expression in smoking cigarettes and drinking alcohol against their parents' wishes. A properly loved child, though, is unlikely – even at this stage –to be so recklessly self-destructive as to take other drugs merely to defy his parents.

I think parents, these days, can confidently expect that their children will receive appropriate instruction against drug abuse from their teachers at school. Parents can complement the instruction their children receive at school by sympathetically talking them through their fluctuating moods, and assuring them that these will subside in due course, but are meanwhile best accepted and tolerated as the chief sign of their burgeoning sexual maturity.

(See also **Addiction, Control.**)

Dyslexia

Dyslexia is the term used to describe the condition of 'word blindness', which handicaps a child in learning to read, write, and spell, notwithstanding his or her normal intelligence. There is still considerable contention amongst physicians and psychologists about whether dyslexia actually exists as a real physical disorder (associated with specific but minimal brain damage), or whether it is a psychological dis-ease.

By all means seek a clear diagnosis and appropriate help for your child if you suspect he or she is dyslexic, but beware offering the child a label – 'I've got dyslexia' – to be used as a blanket justification for under-achieving and withdrawing from the hurly-burly of healthy competitiveness.

(See also **Competitiveness, Handicaps, Illness.**)

Eating

Eating, for all human beings, should be one of the greatest pleasures in life. Most babies and young children naturally want to eat less than most (especially first-time) parents think they 'should' want to. (And most older children want to eat more than their parents believe is possible!) Coercing a child to eat more than he or she enthusiastically wants to eat (especially between one and three years of age) predisposes a child to experience eating as an unpleasurable duty for the rest of his or her life. Don't bribe him to eat his meat and vegetables with the promise of pudding, which covertly implies that meat and vegetables are not enjoyable; rather, let him have his pudding, without comment, when he has had enough – however little – of his meat and vegetables. (If you don't like this idea, then don't make puddings!) In general, encourage a child to have a lifelong 'yum yum' attitude to eating by serving him less rather than more than you think he will want, so that he can eagerly ask for more. Eating is not a moral issue, and it is actually inappropriate to say (even positively), 'Good girl for eating up all your dinner.' Much better to say, with a smile, 'Was that delicious?'

While children's (and grown-ups') dislikes of – a few! – particular foods deserve to be respected, I believe that an omnivorous attitude to food (and all good life experiences) should be encouraged. I personally find it socially unacceptable for a child (or adult) to wrinkle up his nose and/or make whiningly rejecting comments about *any* food that is offered him. Rather, he should be taught from a very early age that when offered any food, however much he dislikes it, he simply says, 'No, thank you.' And, at home, if a child refuses the meal his mother has made for him, he should *not* be offered an alternative (unless he is ill). His refusal should be casually accepted as an indication that he is not hungry and can wait till the next meal time to eat. He will not thereby starve!

(See also **Anorexia nervosa, Bulimia, Choices.**)

Emotions (parental)

Generally speaking, the more freely parents express their emotions in the presence of their child, the more freely will the child express his emotions throughout his life. It is also probably healthier for a child to witness his parents bickering from time to time, rather than to perceive their relationship as unrealistically 'perfect'. However, there are three kinds of emotional expressiveness by parents which profoundly traumatize a child and to which, ideally, he should never be subjected.

The first is uncontrolled rage and/or threats of physical harm or abandonment by a parent towards a child. This will make the child permanently insecure in all his relationships and in his relationship to life itself.

The second is verbal or physical violent abusiveness between his parents. This will prompt him, throughout his life, to expect – and get – only similarly abusive relationships for himself.

The third is helpless appeals from the parent to the child, implicitly or explicitly asking the child to pity the parent's unhappiness and to look after the parent as if the child were the parent and the parent the child. This will induce in the child a lifelong burden of sorrow and sadness, and an incapacity to feel himself loveworthy or to accept love from another.

(See also **Abandonment, Child abuse, Happiness, Love, Permissions, Security.**)

Envy

Envy – as contrasted with jealousy, with which it is often confused – is a wholly false and malevolent attitude. Its two premises are, 'What the other person has and I do not, would make me happy', and 'The other person, having what I believe would make me happy, *must* be happier than I am.' When a child expresses envy, these two premises of his or her thinking should be exposed and seen for what they are. Both premises are false, because 'things' do not make people happy, except very briefly. The second premise is doubly false because what makes one person happy may be quite different from what makes another person happy.

(See also **Competitiveness, Jealousy, Rivalry.**)

Fantasy

Fantasy is a function of imagination, a great God-given gift that makes our experience of the world more vivid and joyful. Scratch just a little beneath the surface, and each person's 'reality' can be seen to be quite different from another's by virtue of the multi-varied colours with which we paint our pictures of the world. Children's imaginations are wonderfully free and can teach so much and be so liberating to grown-up minds, which are comparatively shackled by mundane concerns. Relish and join in the fantasies of your child when he or she offers to share them with you. And never call them lying!

(See also **Truthfulness.**)

Fear

All fear is derivative from the fear of death, and because we all must one day die, fear is not eradicable in life. The bottom-line motive for every human being is our own survival, but as early as six to twelve months of age – even though we cannot articulate it verbally – we become aware that our survival and the fulfilment of our derivative desires are dependent on the goodwill of others. And we quickly learn that the bottom-line motive of all others is *their* own survival, so we commit ourselves to the most fundamental negotiation human beings make with one another: 'I'll give you some of what you want if you give me some of what I want.'

However, there is one capacity of the human psyche that transcends the basic selfishness in us all, and that is love. When we love another human being, we care for that other's survival nearly if not quite as much as our own. 'The maternal instinct' manifests the epitome of love – the totally unconditional, selfless love a mother gives, to the extent that she is capable of willingly sacrificing her own life for the life of her child.

Thus it is the instinctual total love that a mother has for her new-born baby that guarantees the baby's survival before he is aware of his vulnerability and the necessity, in general, to 'give' as well as 'take' in order to maintain others' goodwill towards him. But between six and twelve months of age a baby does become aware of his vulnerability, and his fear of abandonment is poignantly evident. From his point of view, at this time, he has lost his mother forever if she is merely out of his sight for a moment, and since it is only *her* love for him that he has experienced as the boundless love he needs to survive, he responds with screaming terror to her even momentary absence. Only very gradually does this fear of separation from mother diminish, and it is not until a (fully-loved) child is about three years of age that he is wholeheartedly convinced that his basic survival needs can and will be met even in the absence of his mother.

The security a child derives in the first three years of his life from the boundless, unconditional love of his parents – and especially from his primary caretaker (usually his mother) – enables him *for the rest of his life* to experience life as essentially *good* and, in due course, to express real selfless love of his own for another. When a child under the age of three experiences any prolonged separation from his mother (or significant withdrawal of her love for him), he is bound *for the rest of his life* to be predisposed to experience life, and himself, as more *bad* than good, and so will be full of fear and incapable of the incompatible opposite of fear, namely love. (The 'love' of children for their parents, or the 'love' expressed by grown-ups who have been seriously deprived of maternal love in the first three years of their lives, is 'cupboard love', that is, *need*. Real love can only be felt and expressed with energy left over after we have become confident of our basic self-sufficiency.)

Parents, being human, are not God, and no parents can – nor should – be lovingly by the side of their child every moment of every day for the first three years of his or her life. This is as unrealistic as seeking to remove *all* fear from a child. This is tantamount to denying the reality of death, which soon enough has to be understood and lived with by the child. Without the explicit fear of death and the purposeful imposition of derivative fears on the child by the parents – such as the fear of cars, of fire, of electric sockets, etc. – the child would, surely, live a very short life indeed! We don't – and shouldn't – want our childen to be fear*less* and ignorant of evil, but we do want them to experience the universe and themselves as *predominantly good*, and other people as predominantly benevolent and loving. This is our true aim in our quest – especially in the first three years of a child's life – to give him a very, very great deal of our bounteous love and presence.

Notwithstanding that a child continues to need, and to know he has, the unique, unconditional love that only parents can give, for at least the first twenty years of his life, as he gains, bit by bit, his self-sufficient autonomy, he also learns the necessity to 'give' as well as 'take' in his relationships with other people. His parents teach him this by withholding their approval of him for 'selfish' ways that are incompatible with his acceptability to other people, even though – and indeed because – they love him so much. The child's response to his parents' withdrawal of approval is fear that they might actually withdraw their love, on which he so depends. In infancy, the withdrawal of his mother's love would mean total abandonment and his own actual death. As he slowly gains his self-sufficient viability, however, the threat of the withdrawal of his parents' love is experienced as less overwhelmingly terrifying, but nonetheless very frightening, to the extent that he knows he still needs them for his psychological, if not his physical, survival in the world. Each stage of a child's development has its own special fear of the withdrawal of the love of his parents, the risk of which he defends himself against in reactions that are universally typical of natural stages of his psychological development. These universally conditioned fears and defences against them are what makes us all 'human'.

From one to three years of age, the fear of abandonment gradually gives way to the fear of retribution, which is defended against by the child with obedience. From three to six years of age, the core fear is of being judged unworthy of love, which is defended against with a mixture of manipulative compliance and aggressive competitiveness. From six to twelve, the child is more concerned with coming to grips with his vulnerability to physical realities rather than his vulnerabilities in intimate relating. His chief fear now is of death, which he defends against with activities by which he seeks, subconsciously, to control the universe. (That is, he is now more likely to fear *things* than people.) From twelve to sixteen, a child fears most the denial of his autonomy and the gratification of his sexual desires, which he defends himself against with rebellion. And in the final stage of his functional maturation, adolescence, the child fears most his incapacity to be self-sufficient enough in the world-at-large, which he defends against by seeking to take from and acquire for himself the power he perceives in his (especially same-sexed) parent.

Fears of particular people or particular things should always be referred to the general kind of fear associated with the child's age, and the child should be reassured in the appropriate general as well as specific ways needed. No parent should allow a child to perceive the parent as more frightening than loving towards him or her, no matter what the child *ever* is or does.

(See also **Phobias, Timidity.**)

Feeding

See **Eating.**

Fighting

Fighting is the unadorned expression of aggression, which is the life-force in us all, that is, the primary motive of self-preservation above all else. Aggression is complemented in life by tenderness, which is a by-product of love. Love, however, has to be learned gradually over the whole course of our development to maturity, so it is un-natural to expect a child never to fight, before he is old enough to have learned ways of productively displacing and sublimating his aggression as well as counteracting it with tenderness. Especially from six to twelve years of age, when, psychologically, the fear of death is prominent, it is appropriate for a child to show his self-esteem through demonstration of his prowess at self-preservation. This age-group is also more prone than any other to fighting because it is the most asexual stage in the whole of development (from three years onwards). Inasmuch as our basic life-energy is comprised of aggression and sexuality, while sexuality is developmentally suppressed, there is bound to be a corresponding increase in the expression of aggression. For biological reasons, it is generally the case that boys are most inclined to express aggression in physical combat, and girls in psychological viciousness.

(See also **Aggression, Bullying, Quarrelling.**)

Firmness

Say what you mean, and mean what you say. *Do not make threats you know you will not carry out.* You lose by becoming a *liar* in your child's eyes, and losing all real control over him, and you also give your child implicit permission to become a liar himself.

Making meaningless threats and/or 'giving in' to a child is an act of expediency on the part of the parent and, in the long run, expediency never works. Its opposite is patient and wholehearted attention to the problem at hand, until that problem is resolved. Expediency postpones the resolution of a problem, which problem will come back again and again and again . . . until it is properly attended to. Patient and wholehearted attention ensures that *that* problem will not recur.

(See also **Control, Flexibility, Threats.**)

Flexibility

Flexibility is a valuable and endearing characteristic in any human being. Paradoxically, it can only exist in a person who is also extremely self-disciplined and self-controlled, because flexibility implies an ability to tolerate some degree of uncertainty. This ability in turn is dependent on a background of deep security based on general order, control, and predictability in a person's life.

Flexibility in a parent's attitudes and behaviour towards a child is very different from unloving, lazy permissiveness, which may righteously mask itself as flexibility – which it is not.

A child is largely incapable of appreciating or coping with much flexibility at least until the age of about three, by which time a well-brought-up child has achieved a considerable degree of security through the controls imposed on him from the age of about one.

After the age of three, parents may gradually introduce the child to flexibility, through their own *occasional* bending of the firm rules they usually impose – for example, staying up a bit late one night in order for the child to see a loved visitor, having a piece of chocolate just before lunch as 'a special treat', 'skipping' bathtime on an occasion when the child gets home late and exhausted and ready for bed.

When in doubt, err on the side of *in*flexibility. Your child will be the more secure – and therefore happier – for it.

(See also **Conscience, Control, Firmness, Lying, Permissiveness, Routine.**)

Friends

Most parents at some time find themselves 'disapproving' of a friend their child has made, and are prompted to tell the child this and discourage the continuance of the friendship. However, it is important for parents to realize that no friendships between people – children or adults – are arbitrary. There is always a significant meaning and value in any intimate relationship formed between people, no matter how implausible the relationship may appear to be at a superficial, face-value level. By all means express your disapproval of *behaviour* you don't like in your child's friend, but also encourage your child to tell you – if she can – what it is she most likes about this particular friend. This may provide you with some deep understanding of your child and her emotional needs that you didn't before realize.

If you are nonetheless deeply concerned that your child's friend is a truly bad influence on her, diplomatically tell your child's friend's parents about your concern that *both* your children are behaving in disturbing ways that you feel sure upset the other parent as much as you. See if you can join forces – parent to parent – to modify the undesirable influence your children have on each other. Better this than forcibly breaking up the friendship, which is a cruel thing to do and should only be considered as a very last resort.

(See also **Companions, Loneliness, Sociability.**)

Frustration

The frustration as well as the fulfilment of our desires is an unavoidable aspect of being alive. For the first few months of our lives our loving parents appropriately do their utmost to fulfil *all* our desires and minimize our frustration. Thereafter, in the interests of our self-preservation and socialization – and the sanity of our parents, who also have desires! – we are more and more bound to accept, with good grace, that we cannot always have what we want – at least now. Civilization is dependent on us all largely suppressing our infantile screaming reactions to frustration. Although there is a residual 'infant' in each of us, it is rarely – depending on how 'civilized' we are – expressed with uncontrolled vehemence.

(See also **Anger, Control, Temper-tantrums.**)

Generosity

Observation suggests that generosity is at least partly a happy endowment of temperament, as well as of character – that is, innate as well as conditioned. To the extent that generosity can be inculcated in a child, it will be done much more effectively by example than by exhortation.

(See also **Permissions, Possessiveness, Sharing.**)

Gifted children

It should be every child's birthright to have his or her special abilities discovered and nourished, and most loving parents do discover and nourish their children's gifts, and are rightly pleased and proud of them.

Nevertheless, our own or our children's 'gifts' are, by definition, nothing we or they can take credit for. I think it is important for parents to emphasize to their children that they should be grateful for, rather than proud of, their gifts, and, in gratitude, to feel obliged to work hard to fulfil the potential of their gifts and give pleasure to others through them.

I believe that the attributes in ourselves that we are entitled to be most proud of are those of joyful acceptance of what life brings us, and loving kindness towards others, which attributes we may all – gifted or not – choose or not choose to develop in ourselves.

(See also **Competitiveness, Handicaps.**)

God

Whether or not God exists, mankind was bound to have invented Him, to reassure ourselves that pain and death – which are our lot –

have meaning and value beyond our immediate understanding, and 'everything will be all right in the end'. While grown-ups are entitled to be atheists, agnostics, cynical nihilists . . . or anything else that makes God redundant, parents have a *duty* to give their child a positive, optimistic attitude to life, and they have *no right* to impose a negative, pessimistic attitude to life on him.

God, as imaged in the mind of a child, having a long white beard and sitting on a throne in the sky, is an enormously comforting, concrete reality – a super-duper parent who, by definition, goes on looking after the child, even when, *in extremis*, his own mortal parents do not. Tell your young child about God – without any sceptical qualifications, no matter how irreligious you may be – for the sake of his deep psychological need of Him. Your child will have plenty of opportunities later to renounce God, if he wants to, but give him God when he is young, to make his universe benevolent and complete.

(See also **Fear, Good and evil.**)

Good and evil

Abstract a concept as it is, 'good versus evil' is a construct that develops very early in the human mind. It is probably a 'wired-in' response that enables us to make sense of pain, which is the fundamental 'bad' we all experience, from birth, and throughout our lives. A young child implicitly assesses the potential of all new experiences as 'good' ('that which will bring me pleasure') or 'evil' ('that which will bring me pain') long before he or she is capable of the moral judgements that are typically associated with 'good' and 'evil' in grown-up minds.

The essential responsibility of parents towards their child in the matter of good and evil is to convince the child that, while it is true that there is 'evil' (that which causes pain), 'good' (that which causes pleasure) overwhelmingly predominates in the world and in other people. Communicating this to a young child in a 'just-right' way is one of the tightropes that parents have to walk in the healthy rearing of a child. A toddler, for example, is quite right to fear the sea and some dogs, and adults who seek to overcome such fears in a child by denial of the potential 'evil' are telling the child a lie. This will induce in him a predisposition to mistrust and disbelief in general, and a particular inclination to see 'hidden evil' in what he is told is, or superficially appears to be, 'good'.

Timidity in the face of a new experience which *may* cause pain should, in the first instance, be applauded in a child as an intelligent response. Thereafter, in truthfulness and quiet confidence, a parent needs to demonstrate in his or her own unfrightened behaviour that the child's fear is groundless, *or* that, yes, there is something 'bad' to fear, but that that bad can be destroyed, and safety assured, by the relevant precautions.

Traditional children's fairy tales and stories are the most powerful source of feeding a child's overwhelming desire to know about 'good and evil', and to experience 'good' as always triumphing in the end.

(See also **Fear, Death, God, Magic, Timidity.**)

Gratitude

The relationship between children and their parents is not symmetrical. *Children have no cause to be grateful to their parents; parents have much cause to be grateful to their children.* The love and care that parents bestow on a child are the child's birthright; the joy and meaning that a child adds to his or her parents' lives are blessings bestowed on the parents. Parents owe their children everything; children owe their parents nothing. Yet, paradoxically, parents who are satisfied with loving their children as its own reward will, in the course of time, be spontaneously and freely loved by their grown-up children. Parents who expect or demand gratitude from their children are likely, in the course of time, to be resented and avoided by their grown-up children.

(See also **Guilt.**)

Grief

Grief is our natural response, throughout our lives, to the loss of someone we love. Mature acceptance of loss is a lifelong task that we never fully achieve; the bottom-line being death and our raging against it.

Under the age of about five, a child has not yet achieved a realistic understanding of death nor a capacity really to love another person, so the loss of a loved person will be experienced simply as terrifying abandonment, rather than the more sophisticated emotion of grief.

Over the age of about five, a child experiences grief in much the same way as an adult, so I believe that – like an adult – he should be permitted and encouraged fully to express his grief, including attendance at the funeral of someone he has loved. Many grown-ups have told me how angry they now feel for having been kept away from the funeral of a loved relative when they were children. They felt they were prevented from naturally discharging their grief, and 'completing' their relationship to the person who died.

(See also **Abandonment, Death, Depression, Separation.**)

Guilt

'Feeling guilty' is the punishment we inflict on ourselves for having sinned against an aspect of our morality. But, notwithstanding contrary appearances, most guilt is actually a disguised form of righteousness, because it enables the sinner to avoid making reparation for the sin. That is 'feeling guilty' is presumed by many people to *be* the reparation – which it is not. The healthy alternative to guilt is responsibility. This transcends evaluations of good and evil, right and wrong, or better and worse, in favour of being willing to experience ourselves as playing a part in everything that 'happens' to us and to other people in our dealings with them. In 'feeling guilty' we impute powerlessness to ourselves. In feeling responsible we grant ourselves the power continuously to make things the way we want them to be.

Being human, we are all caught up in the stumbling blocks of our quest for righteousness and its attendant, guilt. The greatest privilege of parenthood is that it facilitates us in maturing beyond merely defending our own righteousness in favour of appreciating the value of our power and responsibility.

(See also **Apologizing, Conscience, Morality, Righteousness.**)

Habits

For children and grown-ups alike, habits play a very important part in all our lives. Habits enable us to function automatically in very large areas of our lives without our having to waste time and energy thinking. Some habits are intrinsically supportive of our general well-being, such as those most grown-ups have and seek to instil in their children: looking left, right, and left again before crossing the road; locking the front door before going to bed; cleaning our teeth at fixed times of the day. Many habits have no particular merit, but are just idiosyncratic patterns of behaviour we each have that gives us a pleasant feeling of stability and structure in our lives – from having a gin and tonic every evening before dinner, or reading the newspaper over breakfast, to going to the supermarket at a particular time on a particular day every week.

A few habits are harmful to us, although they provide us with the same deep sense of structure in our lives as our good or harmless habits, and so are very difficult to break. The most common harmful habit in grown-ups is probably cigarette smoking, and in children thumb-sucking, which can, in time, distort the healthy alignment of a child's teeth.

For a child (or grown-up) to be able to give up a habit readily she has to become convinced that her *life will be just as enjoyable without the habit*. I personally think the approach that works best is along the lines of, 'See what it's like going to sleep tonight without sucking your thumb. I think you think you *have* to suck your thumb to be able to go to sleep, but I bet you don't. It would be wonderful if you stopped, so see if you can.' And on any occasion when the child does stop – even for one night – make sure you help him create the new habit of not sucking his thumb by giving him abundant expressions of approval and pride for his achievement.

(See also **Compulsions, Nail biting.**)

Handicaps

We are all born with both handicaps and talents: that is, every human being is 'above-average' in some attributes and abilities and every human being is 'below-average' in some other attributes and abilities. I profoundly believe that the number and extent of our handicaps and talents has nothing whatsoever to do with the happiness we experience in life. It is rather as if we are all 'dealt a hand' – as in a game of cards – and how much we enjoy the game depends on how willing we are to make the most and the best rather than the worst and the least of all the cards in our hands. A fistful of court cards that ensures a 'grand slam' without effort can be entirely devoid of pleasure in the playing; just as a hand with no court cards at all can be played with great skill and satisfaction.

No child – or adult – should be insulted with pity or patronage for his or her handicaps, but rather encouraged to *derive a talent out of his handicap*. Thus a child who has a scaringly painful family life may heal herself through becoming a welfare officer or psychotherapist; a stammerer an orator; a deaf child a teacher of the deaf; a child with a facial blemish a beautician or plastic surgeon. While it is obviously misery-making for anybody to be consumed with an ambition that it is clearly impossible for him to achieve – nobody who is five feet tall is going to be an Olympic high-jumper – every child should be encouraged to aim for that which may be *nearly* impossible, if that is what would bring him the deepest possible satisfaction.

It is the people who know themselves to be handicapped in some way – physically or psychologically – and are passionately committed to healing their own wounds (and, in the process, healing others who are similarly handicapped), who often experience the deepest possible satisfaction with life.

(See also **Dependency, Gifted children, Worrying about your child.**)

Happiness

Apart from continuous loving care, a parent's own happiness is the greatest gift he or she can bestow on his or her child. Children model themselves and their attitudes to life by imitating their parents, and much more so from what their parents *are* than from what their parents say. Feel entitled to happiness, and so will your children.

(See also **Imitation, Permissions.**)

Hate

As love is experienced as passionate positive feeling, hate is experienced as passionate negative feeling. Love and hate are the two sides of all passionate involvement with another, and cannot exist without each other, any more than 'left' can exist without 'right' or 'up' without 'down'. *Because* they love each other, children also sometimes hate their parents, and parents sometimes hate their children. Brothers and sisters also love and hate each other.

Love and hate exist in the human heart like good and evil exist in people and the world, and just as it is vitally important for a child to be convinced that good will always triumph over evil, so he needs to be convinced that love (in himself and others) will always triumph over hate. A child's parents' constant love for him is *the* most tangible evidence that love is paramount in the universe, so it is not to be recommended that parents give voice to their fleeting feelings of hate for their child. However, I believe there are far worse things than, in response to a child's exasperating recalcitrance and 'I hate you', a parent responding 'And I hate you, too.' Far, far worse is a verbal or non-verbal response from the parent that says, 'What a terrible thing to feel', 'After all I've done for you . . .', or – perhaps worst of all – 'That really *hurts* me.' This implies that the child has power, through his behaviour or the expression of his authentic feelings, to harm the well-being or self-esteem of his parents. This also induces in him a feeling of guilt towards his parents, which is at the core of all our neurotic disorders throughout our lives.

When children express hate for each other – just let them. When a child expresses hate for you, his parent, although it is imperative that you do not express 'hurt', it is cruelly discounting of the child's intensely experienced feelings of the moment to imply that his feelings have no effect on you whatsoever. So the response to aim for is something along the lines of, 'I'm sorry you feel like that, but perhaps you'll like me better tomorrow.'

(See also **Discipline, Guilt.**)

Homosexuality

It seems to be the case that there are some people who are born to be homosexual, irrespective of any conditioning to the contrary, and some people who are born to be heterosexual, notwithstanding any conditioning to the contrary. Nevertheless, there is abundant evidence that a child's family experiences, especially between the ages of three and six, are – for the vast majority of people – overwhelmingly influential in determining his or her adult sexual orientation.

Homosexuality in adult life is *biologically* abnormal. It is a social handicap, to be avoided, if possible, by each child being encouraged clearly, from the age of three onwards, to identify with his or her same-sexed parent and being denied too close and possessive an intimacy with his or her opposite-sexed parent.

(See also **Custody, Sexism, Sexuality, Three to six.**)

Hospitalization

Happily, over the past twenty or thirty years, society at large has become increasingly aware of the overwhelmingly traumatizing sense of abandonment that a young child experiences when separated from his mother for even a few days, and especially when added to the usually traumatizing experience of being in hospital. Thus it is now common practice for mothers routinely to stay with their child and sleep alongside him when he is in hospital. This is as it always should be, although when there are other children at home to care for it is not always possible. Whatever the case, parents need to be aware that, regardless of a young child's apparent easy acquiescence to being hospitalized, the truth is that the separation from his mother is extremely disturbing of his psychological well-being, and is far, far more painful to him than any of the surgical or medical procedures he has to endure.

As a rule of thumb, it is wisest to avoid any hospitalization that is not urgently necessary for a child before he is at least three – and preferably six – years old, by which time he is able to tolerate a few days' separation from his mother without severe, and difficult to repair, psychological stress.

(See also **Abandonment, Anxiety, Fear, Separation.**)

House-moving

Quite apart from the sheer physical work involved for the grown-ups, house-moving is also psychologically a very stressful experience for grown-ups and children alike. Our deepest sense of well-being in the physical world is secured by the familiarity and safe privacy of 'home', where everything is ordered in just the way that suits our needs. House-moving tears up that order, and creates temporary chaos in our lives, which is extremely stressful even to the most self-sufficient grown-ups (notwithstanding the positive excitement that may also be associated with the move).

A young child is not able to appreciate or anticipate – as adults are – the advantages and pleasures of his new home. All he knows is that his present precious home (which is even more central a component of his physical universe than it is to his parents) is being dissembled. He is likely to show signs of psychological disturbance – such as regressing to 'babyish' behaviour – from the time he knows about the impending move until at least several weeks after the move, when he has become convinced that stable order has been restored.

Most parents instinctively send a child to stay with grandma (or some other loved and trusted caretaker) on the actual day of the move – as much for their own sakes as his! – and it is certainly a very good idea to save him the anguish of witnessing the final dismantling of the house – especially his own room.

In the new house, give the creation of order and familiarity in the child's bedroom first priority, and reassure him repeatedly that 'we won't move again for a very, very long time'.

If at all possible, avoid any house-moving when a child is between about one and two years of age. Under about one, the security a child needs is overwhelmingly from the physical presence of his mother, and has little to do with the familiarity of his physical environment, and over the age of two, he is capable of some understanding of the nature and meaning of the move. But between one and two he has become powerfully attached to 'home', and yet is too young to be anything but terrified of its change.

For children of all ages (and their parents) it is best, if possible, to avoid moving at times when the child has other unavoidable stresses, such as exams, to contend with.

(See also **Routine.**)

Hyperactivity

Some children – and adults – are naturally and normally more restless and/or more nervous than others. These characteristics usually come under the heading 'hyperactivity'. Whether or not a child has a medically definable condition that warrants this label, it is of no value at all to the child to be offered it as a description of himself. Such a label is harmful to the child in two ways: it implicitly defines him as irremediably 'bad' and, at the same time, gives him the liberty always to behave 'hyperactively' because he has been given to understand he 'can't help it'.

A parent should think positively instead about the 'hyperactive' traits in her child, labelling him – if she must label him at all – as very energetic and sensitive, and helping him find constructive and self-esteem-boosting activities to absorb his energy.

To the extent that hyperactivity can be an abnormal condition in a child, there is evidence that it is to some extent attributable to the child's allergic sensitivity to artificial colourings and/or sweeteners in food. When these substances are eliminated from such a child's diet, his symptoms subside.

(See also **Handicaps.**)

Illness

All children are nearly inevitably bound to suffer bouts of colds, sore throats, earaches, and other infectious diseases of childhood, in the process of gaining the degree of immunity that most grown-ups have achieved.

When a child is ill – whether the illness is slight or serious – a parent's attitude to the illness can have a marked effect on the speed of the child's recovery and on the frequency of illness in the child in future.

While it is undeniable that bacterial and viral infections are 'real', and that some children are constitutionally more vulnerable to infections than others, it is also the case that mental attitudes play an important part in determining any individual's vulnerability to infection and the speed of recovery from any given illness. Children (and adults) are more prone to illnesses of all kinds, and take longer to recover from them, if they have been *encouraged* to be ill by parents who give them significantly more love and attention when they are ill than when they are not. This is not to say that people should not be given tender loving care when they are ill. They should, of course, but it behoves parents scrupulously to examine their own motives and make sure that they do not actually relish the added dependency of their child when he is ill. This could covertly communicate to the child that they enjoy loving and nurturing his comparative helplessness when ill more than they enjoy loving and nurturing him when he is well and comparatively independent. Any child who receives such (covert) messages will come to presume that he can get love best by being ill (and dependent), and he *will* be ill more often than most people for the rest of his life.

I observed some unambiguous testimony of the influence of the mind on bodily disease in one of my daughters when she was between eight and ten. We had neighbours with a daughter about the same age as mine. The two girls did not like each other, but felt bound by social convention to invite each other to their birthday parties. For three years in a row, on the day of the girl-next-door's birthday party, my daughter woke up with a sore throat and a temperature. Our doctor confirmed that she had a 'real' sore throat and a 'real' temperature which, of course, fully justified her in not going to the party.

Body and mind are inextricably linked in all of us, and it is valuable to remind ourselves that 'disease' is actually *dis-ease*.

(See also **Bravery, Comforting, Dependency.**)

Imagination

See **Fantasy.**

Imitation

All young children believe their parents are the most wonderful people in the world. So do all older children, at the deepest level of their being, notwithstanding that they often declare the opposite in word and deed! Naturally, therefore, a child imitates her parents in her bid to be as wonderful as they are. There is no greater power on earth than that automatically bestowed on people when they become parents; the hand that rocks the cradle rules the world.

Children incorporate into their own selves the ways their parents *are* much more than the ways their parents exhort them to be. Ideally, parents' exhortations to their children match their ways of being, but if any of what you exhort your child to be or do has the flavour of 'Do as I say, not as I do', you can be sure she will see through your hypocrisy and discount your exhortations. Actions speak louder than words, and your actions are the model on which your child bases her own.

(See also **Happiness, Permissions.**)

Incest

The incest taboo is universal, and is understood to have its roots in biology. That is, mankind seems to understand implicitly that miscogenation or interbreeding leads to greater evolutionary vigour than inbreeding, or the mixing of too-similar genes. So, derivatively, there is normally a felt revulsion towards the idea of marrying a close relative. This is interestingly reflected in children brought up on kibbutzes, who typically have as close an intimacy with all the other children on the kibbutz as they do with their own brothers and sisters. When they grow up, I am told, they virtually never marry each other.

Paradoxically, however, the members of our immediate family are also the first objects of our sexual desire, and incestuous fantasies and impulses are experienced in all families – between parents and children, between brothers and sisters and, not infrequently between uncles and nieces, aunts and nephews, and grandparents and their grandchildren.

Healthily, morality and propriety win over incestous impulses that grown-ups feel towards children. Children, in their greater vulnerability, seem usually, from puberty onwards, to have an inbuilt added defence against their incestuous impulses, namely a conscious feeling of physical *revulsion* towards their opposite-sexed parent and their opposite-sexed siblings. (My own observation is that the degree of revulsion a pubescent child feels towards his or her opposite-sexed parent mirrors the degree of underlying attachment the child previously achieved in that relationship.) Only very gradually, as children achieve emotional and sexual security with appropriate partners of their own, does the revulsion they feel towards their opposite-sexed parent dissolve, and they become once again able to express love for their opposite-sexed parent with some degree of spontaneous *physical* affection.

When the defences against incest break down and there is actual sexual contact between parents and children or between brothers and sisters (when either are over the age of about ten), the psychological consequences for a child are almost always *horrendous*, leading to intense pain, shame, guilt, deep general unhappiness, and an inability to form lasting loving relationships for the rest of the child's life.

Some sex play between brothers and sisters (as well as between children and their friends) in their pre-pubescent years is normal, although between brothers and sisters I think it is best gently discouraged. By about the age of ten, it is important that brothers and sisters do not share a bedroom.

(See also **Child abuse, Custody, Sexuality.**)

Independence

The whole of our development, from birth to maturity, consists of gaining ever-increasing independence. At core, the task of child-rearing is for parents to make themselves increasingly redundant to the child's needs.

As every new stage of independence in a child is approached, parents are faced with the tricky task of judging just the right balance between stretching the boundaries of the child's timidity, while also avoiding the undoing of some of his already achieved ways of being independent by too-hasty a precipitation into new ways.

Broadly speaking, a child under the age of about six needs to be more pushed than held back from new forms of independence: 'Go on, stroke the dog, it's friendly.' From six to twelve (the most 'sensible' stage of development), the child's own inclinations towards greater independence typically match his parents' expectations of him: 'Can I join the Boy Scouts?' 'Of course you can'. From twelve to sixteen, his parents face the awesome task of needing often to hold him back from forms of independence that he demands but is not yet ready for: 'No, you can't go away camping with your girlfriend on your own.' In the final stage of adolescence, parents are called on to respond appropriately as their child oscillates uncertainly between having 'no need whatsoever for his parents' care or guidance' and demanding to be cared for and cossetted in ways he has not needed for years, when he retreats, bruised, from some of his encounters in the grown-up world: 'Yes, of course I want you to lead your own life in your own way. But I want you to be *really* ready to leave home before you do so. How about going on living here for another six months before finding your own place, and then you can go with my wholehearted blessing?'

(See also **Birth order, Bribery, Dependence, Leaving home, Protectiveness, Responsibilities, Regression.**)

Insecurity

Insecurity in a child is always emotional rather than material. Insecurity in children is produced by parental neglect, and the experience of the child that his life is chaotic and frighteningly unpredictable. The amount of money spent on a child is utterly irrelevant to his sense of security or insecurity. The material privileges of a neglected child of well-to-do parents in no way mitigate his insecurity. If he is deprived of the loving presence and attention of his parents that are his birthright, he hurts just as badly and becomes as desperately greedy for love as the poorest child who lives in a slum, if that child also is fundamentally unloved. The love or lack of love given us by our parents in childhood is all that essentially determines how secure or insecure we feel and, ulti-mately, how happy or miserable will be our lives.

(See also **Anxiety, Clingingness.**)

Intelligence

See **Curiosity, Language, Learning.**

Intimacy

Intimacy is the expression of free, spontaneous, truthful, non-damaging closeness between people. It is the ideal form of interac-tion between all people because it gives us our times of greatest happiness. But being intimate with others also makes us excru-ciatingly vulnerable to the deep pain that may be inflicted on us by others if they choose so to use the knowledge of us we have given them. So intimacy involves risk, and many people, sadly, deeply presume that if others know them intimately they are bound to be hurt and rejected by them. As a result, many people are frightened of intimacy and never allow others to get really close to them.

Thus people's overall willingness to be intimate with others depends on the general level of *trust* they have that those others are essentially benevolent towards them. The ability to trust others derives from the *unconditional love* given an individual as a child by his or her parents, especially up to the age of three.

(See also **Incest, Love, Manners, Modesty, Rejection, Separation, Sexuality, Sociability.**)

Jealousy

Like envy, jealousy is an unhappy desire to possess what somebody else has got. Envy is for some *thing* another has got, jealousy is for some *love* another has got. Envy is *always* false and wholly malevolent. Jealousy may be false and malevolent as well – when it is objectively unfounded – but often is a natural response to a loved person withdrawing love from oneself in favour of another.

A fully mature grown-up (which few of us ever are!) realizes that love is not like chocolate cake – divisible into smaller and smaller portions the more people there are to share it. Love is limitlessly expandable, so that somebody who loves us may also love others without the love for ourselves being withdrawn or diminished. Parents learn this truth to their own surprise when they discover that they love their second child every bit as much as their first, even though they go on loving their first child as much as ever before.

But however true this principle may actually be, we are, throughout our lives, acutely vulnerable to the mundane reality that – except for the love we have for our children – we do tend to be very fickle in all our loves. And – at least in the realm of loving sexual intimacy – very few of us truly believe in our partner's (or our own) capacity wholeheartedly to love more than one person at a time. If our partner expresses love for somebody else, this immediately implies to us that he or she has ceased to love us, our self-esteem plummets, and we are thrown into the agony of jealousy, even if we are truly assured by our partner that this new love in no way diminishes his or her love for ourselves.

No wonder, then, that a child, too, feels acutely jealous of the love his adored parents give to their other children, notwithstanding the parents' reassurance to their children that they love each of them limitlessly.

First children inevitably experience greater jealousy than subsequent children, because of their perception of their parents' love being taken away from them as it is given to a later-born brother or sister. Second and subsequent children have an enormous advantage over first children in having no experience of *exclusive* parental love for themselves. As a result, they have the wisdom from birth – which first children may poignantly struggle to achieve all their lives – that 'I can be fully loved, even though the person who loves me also fully loves another.' (However this by no means makes second and subsequent children immune from jealousy for their parents' love.)

But, notwithstanding the deep truth, maturely understood by fully self-confident grown-ups, that jealousy is destructive and unnecessary, there is something 'inhuman' in those (rare) people who honestly claim never to feel jealous. There is an implied arrogance in their utterly self-confident invulnerability, and we – rightly, I think – like them less for it. While we all want for our children a degree of self-confidence and assurance that minimizes their vulnerability to jealousy, we also want them, from time to time, to be prompted to say, 'Perhaps I need to make myself more worthy of the love of another that I so desire', which is, in small doses, endearing humility and the positive side of jealousy.

This positive aspect of jealousy is most obvious in the outcome of a child's jealousy of his or her same-sexed parent for the love of his or her opposite-sexed parent, especially in the critical Oedipal stage of development between three and six years of age. When, for whatever reason, a child does *not* have to face and deal with this jealousy of his or her same-sexed parent, the outcome is a serious incapacity to *earn* the love of another in grown-up life.

A first child's jealousy of the next-born is poignantly acute, but careful handling, from the time of the second child's birth, can keep it within healthy bounds. Exploit the new-born's incomprehension by confiding, sighingly, to the first-born, what a 'nuisance' the new baby is when she cries or otherwise demands attention, when you would 'much rather' be talking to or playing with or reading to your older child. As far as the first child is concerned, at least for the first two or three months after the second child is born, let him see you experience your ministering to the needs of the baby as much more a duty than a pleasure, and save most of your 'beyond-the-call-of-duty' kissing of and cooing at the baby for the evening, after your older child is asleep. Don't worry, you won't be harming the baby, and you will be doing a power of good for your older child. An older child's jealousy of a new-born baby is avoidable; an older child's jealousy of a baby once the baby becomes 'cute' from about nine months onwards, is inevitable. But if, during the first weeks and months of the baby's life, you have exhibited sensitive and purposeful 'favouritism' towards the older child, you will have done much to mitigate the older child's jealousy and to ensure an essentially loving relationship between the children for the rest of their lives.

(See also **Competitiveness, Only child, Rivalry, Spacing of children.**)

Language

Although a child does not actually begin to use speech until the second year of her life, her most lasting and important acquisition of language is actually in the first year of her life when, through the smiles and frowns and multitudinous other grimaces and tones of voice and inflections that loving parents instinctively bombard her with, she learns the vocabulary of *non-verbal communication*, which constitutes at least 90 per cent of all the meaning in even the most grown-up transactions between people. And even in the matter of speech itself, although she has not yet herself *uttered* any of the sounds she has heard in the language into which she was born, by the time she is one year old, she is already so attuned to her 'native' language that learning the different sounds of another language would already be somewhat 'foreign' to her.

In my work as a psychotherapist I have become poignantly aware that amongst seriously disturbed people one characteristic they nearly all have in common is that they have been denied the experience of learning all the minute movements in face and body that constitute the non-verbal language that contains so much of the meaning of our communications with others. Seriously disturbed people often only 'know' the literal meanings of words alone and this is often the consequence of maternal neglect in their first year of life. The human brain grows more in the first year of life than it does during the whole of the rest of development to maturity.

This is meant to reassure the exhausted mother of a baby that in all her selfless work and effort she is actually being granted the privilege of the greatest possible influential power that one person can ever exert over another.

(See also **Baby-talk.**)

Learning

The intelligence in all of us seeks stimulation and, irrespective of whether a child's natural intelligence is 'above-average', 'average', or 'below-average', he needs and is entitled to the deep satisfaction of learning. The years of childhood are very precious indeed as the unrepeated stage in our lives when our biological programming determines that we are overwhelmingly willing and able to learn. And what we learn in childhood is retained by us more powerfully and lastingly than will ever again be possible. Stimulate and flatter your child by stretching his intelligence; and do not baulk at imposing on him *rote* learning – arithmetical tables, reams of beautiful poetry . . . or what you will – the gifts of which will then be his or hers for life.

(See also **Curiosity, Language.**)

Leaving home

On average, a child needs to begin leaving home at about age eighteen. I say 'begin' because the emotional process of making the radical detachment from the parents associated with no longer living with them usually takes a few years to complete. (The typical British pattern of eighteen year olds pursuing tertiary education in places other than their home-town is a useful external structure students are granted that enables them to have 'left home' during term-time and yet to 'return home' during vacations, in a natural way that avoids any loss of face for them.) By about age twenty-two (which happily typically coincides with the completion of a four-year course of tertiary study), the child should be capable of making the final severance of his umbilical attachment to his parents' home and creating his own domestic environment. Parents can know their child has attained psychological adulthood when he or she calls his own, rather than his parents', address 'home'.

If the overall development of the child has been seriously hampered by any abnormality of events or circumstances in previous years, the impact of these may be felt in a young adult's inability willingly to leave his or her parents' home. He or she is likely to find justifiable excuses, such as the high cost of rented accommodation, unemployment, or whatever, but he is actually deeply demanding – albeit often unconsciously – to finish his 'unfinished business' with his parents before he can become the self-sufficient adult they now expect him to be. In such cases it behoves parents – for the sake of their own desire for independence from their child, as well as his from them – to accept responsibility for the underlying pathology in the child, whose symptom is his clinging to living with them. At this stage it is often useful to enlist the help of a competent psychotherapist to uncover the nature of the 'unfinished business' and to facilitate the child and his parents in successfully working through it.

Parents who collude with or passively accept unhealthy clinging of their adult child out of their own unwillingness to face 'the empty nest' and move forward to a new stage in their own lives, will pay the price of an ever-increasing resentfully hostile relationship with that child who, when he finally breaks free, may feel impelled to cut himself off from them completely.

Parents and children who healthily face the poignancy of the children leaving home in early adult life are typically surprised and happily rewarded a few years later with a *new* close intimacy that develops between them, especially when the children make their parents grandparents.

(See also **Independence, Protectiveness, Responsibilities.**)

Loneliness

Loneliness is the obverse of the capacity to be happily alone. Healthily, we all regularly need and enjoy being with other people at some times, and regularly need and enjoy being alone at other times. People are temperamentally different from each other in the proportions of their time they prefer being with other people and being alone. Do not expect your child necessarily to be as you are in this regard. Respect his innate temperament.

However, irrespective of innate temperamental differences between people, all children should, ideally, be taught to adapt their temperamental differences in an accepting way to varying external conditions. A naturally solitary child needs to be taught to accept that there are some occasions when he is obliged to be sociable; and a naturally gregarious child needs to be taught to accept that there are some occasions when he has to be alone and, nonetheless, able to enjoy himself.

When a child is explicitly lonely by virtue of being ostracized by

other children, something is seriously amiss in his ways of inter-
acting with people. This needs urgent attention, or else he will carry
his social handicap with him into his adult life, by which time his
capacity to learn adaptive new ways of socializing is greatly diminished. If you are unable to see any obvious reason why other children shun your child, in the first instance consult his teacher, who will
probably have some useful insights to offer you. Naturally, parents
lovingly think well of their own children, but parents also need to
have the courage to face and deal with the reality – if necessary –
that their child has some unacceptable traits that need correcting if
other children are to want to be his friends.

(See also **Companions, Friends, Sociability.**)

Love

Love has many parameters, but the most important one in the
relationship between parents and children is that it is not symmetrical. We are not born capable of loving; we learn how to love
through the example of the love that is gratuitously bestowed on us
by our parents. The ease or difficulty with which we are able to form
loving relationships in grown-up life is directly consequential on the
ways our parents loved us throughout our childhoods. If our parents
loved us well, so will we love well. If our parents loved us badly, we
will have to struggle long and hard in grown-up life to love other
people, including our own children, well. A child who is badly-
loved does not, when grown-up, love his parents. He is also likely to
be full of unwholesome guilt towards them, which represents his
deeply repressed belief that his parents did not love him well
because he was 'bad' in some way. Thus he has to go on struggling,
futilely, through his guilt, to be 'good' enough to get from them the
love they didn't give him.

*A child is entitled to his parents' love as his birthright; parents have
to earn their child's love.* The apparent 'love' of young children for
their parents is actually *need*, and wise parents know this and do not
falsely flatter themselves that this has value as love. In grown-up
relationships, neediness is an arch enemy of true love, and overly
needy adults have great difficulty forming lasting loving relationships, because their neediness prompts them to ask too much and
give too little. Overly needy adults were children whose parents did
not give them love *freely*; their parents, in one way or another,

expected or demanded that the child give love back to them in a tit-for-tat way, which is neither natural nor possible for a child to do. Needy grown-ups are very unlikely to be able freely to love their own children, and so it may be that 'the sins of the fathers are visited upon the children even unto the third and fourth generation'.

(See also **Guilt, Permissions, Spoiling.**)

Lying

People lie because they fear the consequences if the truth be known. When a child lies to his parents he fears their punishment of him for the truth he is seeking to hide from them. Whatever the 'crime' the child has committed, the lying about it is the symptom of his consequent fear, so it is important for parents not to convey that the child's lying is an additional crime, which only doubles the child's fear. Instead, tell the child that you think he is lying because he is ashamed of something he has done and is frightened of your retributive anger if you find out. Also tell him that, although, if he has done wrong, you will insist that he accept responsibility for his wrong-doing, there is nothing he can ever do that will stop you loving him – because you are his parents. Quietly persist in extracting the truth from the child and, when it is revealed, continue – quietly – to insist that he make whatever reparation is appropriate for any 'crime' he has committed. Always minimize your anger, shock, disbelief, etc., and maximize your sympathetic understanding of the 'human-ness' of the motive that prompted him to commit the 'crime'. In this way, his fear of you – which is undesirable – will be diminished, and lying to you (which represents his fear of you) is unlikely to occur again.

I believe a child, from the age of about five onwards, is capable of understanding, and should be taught the virtue, additional to truthfulness, of 'white lies'. White lies should be justified as an important means of not hurting somebody else's feelings, through not telling them 'the truth, the whole truth, and nothing but the truth'. Thus, for example, a child deserves praise for thanking somebody for a gift and saying, 'It's lovely', even though she actually loathes whatever it is that has been given her.

(See also **Apologizing, Fantasy, Fear, Manners, Morality, Righteousness, Truthfulness.**)

Magic

A young child's thinking concerning *why* things happen is 'magical'. Only very gradually does magic give way to logic, and it is not, in fact, until a child is about fourteen that she is capable of fully deductive, syllogistic thought.

As grown-ups, even though we expect of ourselves and others that logical, rational thought predominates in our everyday dealings with people and the inanimate world, we all – however secretly – still 'believe in' magic. This is manifest in our superstitions and the multitudinous obsessive-compulsive rituals that, to a greater or lesser extent, influence our everyday thoughts and actions. Even amongst the most proudly rational grown-ups there are none who do not sometimes 'touch wood', feel anxious if some particular self-imposed ritual in their life is disturbed, or 'pray' that something will turn out as they want it to, etc.

Magic, as the means to ward off evil, especially predominates in the minds of six- to twelve-year-old children, even though they are also well on the way to grown-up rationality. Parents can positively exploit this fact by claiming magical omnipotence in themselves (which their child deeply endows them with anyhow!) and 'abracadabra-ing' away their child's fears and phobias. This can be effective for a child even as old as about twelve, who, while the rational part of his mind disbelieves, is still able and willing to allow his irrational mind to be thus calmed. God is the 'magic' that grown-ups substitute for the benevolent omnipotence that children still ascribe to their parents.

(See also **Compulsions.**)

Manners

Manners are *unnatural*, because they are designed to indicate that we are as concerned with other people's well-being as our own – which is not true! But, at the deepest level, our actual survival depends on our effective use of the camouflage of manners, because (good) manners are the implicit way in which we contract with others for them not to savage us and us not to savage them despite the underlying truth that, above all, we are primarily *self*-interested. Because we know that all of the others are primarily self-interested, too, we realize that, without the mediation of good manners, our lives would be overwhelmingly a fearful bid to survive the free aggression of those who see us as in any way an obstacle to the attainment of their selfish ends.

The underlying self-seeking motive in us all is never fully compensated by manners, and the contentment of most people's lives is contaminated with the stress – especially in gainful employment – of needing generally to be on the look-out for the aggression of others. The only quality in human beings that fully negates our essential self-centredness is love, and, by and large, each of us only really loves a very few others. 'Civilization' is directly proportional to the general degree of compulsion in a population of people to behave with 'good manners' towards each other. *Good manners are about behaving lovingly, even when we don't feel loving.*

The imposition of good manners on a child becomes necessary from about one year old, when his aggressive, self-centred motivation, combined with his mobility, are more than parents (or other people) are willing to tolerate in their unbridled form. Happily nature concurs, when a child is one to three years of age, in his parents' aim to socialize him, because this is the age when a child is most inclined to general obedience in the interests of avoiding retribution. Because good manners are 'unnatural', they cannot be acquired, as many other attributes are, by 'one-trial learning'. The demand for good manners has to be reiterated by parents, as a matter of course, over and over again, especially from one to three years of age, until the child *automatically* and virtually *always* says 'Please' and 'Thank you', and doesn't snatch, etc.

Later, from three to six years of age, good manners are reinforced and consolidated by the justifications of morality. If all goes well, by the time a child is about six, his basic good manners are so deeply entrenched in him as to be automatic for the rest of his life.

(However, from twelve to sixteen, the healthy development of a child demands that he be essentially rebellious towards *all* that his parents have taught him to value, and he is naturally extremely bad-mannered. To the extent that a twelve- to sixteen-year-old's behaviour and attitudes generally represent the absolute opposite of everything he knows he 'should' do and be, the more bad-mannered he is, the more good-mannered it can be inferred he 'really' is!)

(See also **Conformity, Sharing.**)

Masturbation

Masturbation is about the sensory pleasure that can be derived from touching one's own genitals. In early childhood it has no specifically sexual connotations, and it is probably wisest for parents to ignore it rather than to reinforce it by even gentle rebuke. However, if a child masturbates in company, it should be stopped in the same way as, say, nose-picking, by telling the child something like, 'It's bad manners to play with your willie/bottom in front of other people, so please don't do it.'

From puberty onwards, masturbation naturally becomes associated with sexual fantasies. It is natural and nearly universal, although some girls do not seem to need to go through this stage in their sexual maturation.

(See also **Sexuality.**)

Modesty

There is a very thin dividing line between unhealthy shame*ful*ness and unhealthy shame*less*ness in all of us. Unhealthy shame*ful*ness makes us over-reticent about our sensuality in general and our sexuality in particular. Unhealthy shame*less*ness reduces our concept of sexuality to a mere appetite, and destroys the possibility of our experiencing sex as the sacred expression of love, in which expression it is the most ecstatic experience available to us in life.

As a rule of thumb, a best balance between shamefulness and shamelessness is probably imbued in a child by giving him permission to be shame*less* up until the age of about three, but to suggest that he also become appropriately shame*ful* from three to six, at which stage he first becomes fully aware of gender distinctions and clearly identifies him- or herself as belonging to one gender or the other.

I personally believe that it is probably best for a child's opposite-sexed parent to avoid exposing his or her nakedness to the child by the time the child is about four. Certainly, by the time a child reaches puberty, he or she will be displaying an instinctive modesty about his or her own body, and although he or she may remain an unabashed witness to the nakedness of his or her same-sexed parent, he or she is likely to be scrupulously modest about displaying his or her own body to his or her same-sexed – let alone opposite-sexed – parent. Parents should respect this modesty in their pubescent child as well as his or her derivative increasing desire for privacy in general.

(See also **Incest, Permissions, Sexuality, Truthfulness.**)

Money

Before the age of about six, money is just a kind of physical object to a child, and her parents' use of it in shops, on buses, etc. invokes a wondrous awe at the 'secret rites' of grown-ups.

From six to twelve, a child knows the uses of money, but does not experience it as a 'problem' as grown-ups so often do. It is more of a 'collectable item', like stamps or scout badges, and the impulse to *save* which is the typical psychological orientation of this stage of development is manifest in the child often having a sizeable bank account.

By puberty, a child experiences money as a universal bartering commodity in much the same way as grown-ups do, and she now wants lots of it, specifically to spend on sexually-motivated self-adornment, and generally to express the impulse to *waste* (which is the natural psychological orientation of this stage of development, in marked contrast to the impulse to *save* in the six to twelve year old). Indeed, to the pubescent, money is the one thing her parents have to give her that she admits to actually wanting from them; so for the parents of a twelve- to sixteen-year-old, the withholding of pocket money is often the only real power they have over the child in their struggle to maintain their tenuous control of the child's rudeness, rebellion, lack of consideration, and general wayward-ness. The child has no 'better nature' at this stage to appeal to, and although loving parents accept their responsibility to 'win' in battles with their child over issues that really matter to them, the withholding of pocket money as a disciplinary sanction is a very useful advantage to them at this, the most testing time of all in the whole task of parenting.

(See also **Adolescence, Six to twelve, Twelve to sixteen.**)

Morality

Morality is learned through the explicit exhortations of parents to their child from three to six years of age. Morality consolidates the child's commitment to good manners, which were imposed on him from one to three years of age. Together, manners and morality provide the necessary counterforce to our instinctual, aggressive self-centredness which, unconstrained, would prevent us relating to most other people most of the time except aggressively. Our morality is polished up and refined in adolescence through awareness, developed at this stage, that morality is 'larger than' the law of the land, and is also a realm of attitudes and actions quite separate from and independent of reason.

I believe it is an essential responsibility of parenthood explicitly to teach children that *sexual behaviour is a moral matter, not merely a matter of the avoidance of pregnancy or disease.*

(See also **Adolescence, Character, Conscience, Guilt, Sexuality, Three to six.**)

Nail biting

In the first place, nail biting should be presumed to be a symptom of general anxiety in a child and, if possible, the cause of the anxiety should be uncovered and dissolved. To the extent that it is a residual habit, its elimination can be helped – with the child's permission – by the application of a foul-tasting substance (available from pharmacists) to the child's finger-nails.

(See also **Anxiety, Compulsions, Habits.**)

Nervousness

Some people are naturally more nervous or 'highly strung' than others. To the extent that you recognize your child to be innately more nervous than average, do your best to provide lots of order, structure and routine in her life to counteract and contain her excessive reactivity.

(See also **Anxiety, Fear, Routine, Security.**)

Nightmares

Nightmares – in children and grown-ups alike – can be understood as the manifestation of the universal unconscious knowledge of evil. There are 'baddies' as well as 'goodies' in the universe of the human mind, so we sometimes have nightmares as well as sweet dreams. In comforting a child who has just had a nightmare, it may help him if you suggest that next time he encounters a monster (or any other embodiment of evil) in his dreams, he kills that monster. By this you will be implying that good can triumph over evil, and also that the child himself can manifest the power of good through his own will.

(See also **Death, God, Good and evil, Magic.**)

Obedience

Obedience is about deferring to someone else's greater power. Parents are more powerful than their children, and children know it, so children deeply and implicitly *are* obedient to their parents.

Reflecting on the reality of another's power over us makes us feel humiliated and resentful at the essential unfairness of the inequality between us. This unfair inequality is unavoidable in the relationship between parents and their childen, and children know they have to put up with it until they are grown-up. Thus it is unkind to brutalize a child's tender helplessness further by explicitly demanding, 'Do as I say!' any more than is absolutely necessary. By and large it is only at puberty (when a child prematurely seeks the full autonomy and power of grown-upness by forceful and excessive *dis*obedience towards his or her parents), that it is often appropriate for parents to respond with, 'Because I say so!' or 'Do as you're told, or there'll be no pocket-money/school trip/new dress . . .'

In general, children are as entitled as grown-ups to being allowed a certain amount of *time* to disengage from their present pre-occupations in order to be ready to comply with inter-personal duties. A child – just like a grown-up – is much more likely to be amicably compliant to 'Dinner will be ready in ten minutes' than 'Come to dinner *now* – and hurry up!'

(See also **Bribery, Control, Discipline, Disobedience, Prohibitions, Punishment, Spoiling.**)

Oedipus Complex

See **Three to six.**

Only child

An only child can be profoundly handicapped by virtue of the deprivation of the nearly continuous aggressive and conciliatory experience that brothers and sisters have with each other, which forms the basis of all of our grown-up knowledge about how to get on with other people, *as equals*. Only children are outnumbered by their parents, so they are almost inevitably *over-adapted*. That is, they are nearly always too 'nice', too-good-to-be-true, and may well be 'picked on' by other children at school for this characteristic, while not understanding what they have done to deserve this. Thus they may become even 'nicer' in a bid to overcome the hostility of others, which only exacerbates the situation.

As a grown-up, an only child will have considerable difficulty in assessing the right balance between giving and taking in intimate relationships, and will generally be uncomfortable in sharing attention with others in a group. At a deep level, he will be unable to distinguish between 'play fighting' and real aggression, and so will tend to oscillate between social inhibitedness and unacceptable demandingness. As compensation, an only child will be above-average in his or her understanding of and ability to handle boss-subordinate relationships, our knowledge of which is based on our relationships as children with each of our parents – the experience of which an only child has a super-abundance.

Inasmuch as an only child receives an abundance of nurturance and is not required daily to give nurturance to other children, some compensation for this imbalance can be achieved by giving her a pet whose welfare she is made solely responsible for maintaining. Loving parents may also go a long way towards mitigating the emotional 'blind spot' in their only child by drawing on the 'child' in themselves to have transactions with him that are more typical of behaviour between children than between a parent and a child. For example, sometimes say such things as, 'Go away, I hate you', encouraging him to say, 'I hate you, too.' Be *glad* when he is 'naughty', rebellious, or 'cheeky', and generally *under*-respond to his 'goodness' and 'niceness'.

A child separated by six or more years from his or her nearest brother or sister is effectively an only child.

(See also **Birth order, Jealousy, Quarrelling.**)

Permissions

Permissions are the opposite of inhibitions. Permissions are transmitted by parents to children through *enthusiasm*. While there is some value in explicitly and verbally giving a child various permissions, by far the most potent source of a child's lifelong capacity to *enjoy life* is the parents' own obvious enjoyment of life, which needs no back-up with words. Permissions are essentially about the freedom to be emotionally expressive, and when a child is a witness to his or her parents' pleasure in cooking, reading, gardening, watching television, playing cards . . . the child is likely to have an enhanced capacity for pleasure in these activities for the whole of his or her life. (Research has shown that the overwhelmingly most relevant factor in a five-year-old's ability easily to learn to read is that he or she has been a witness to his or her parents reading for their own pleasure!)

Permission appropriately to express unhappy feelings is also acquired by the child through being witness to his parents' unashamed and spontaneous expressions of grief, anger, disappointment, etc.

(See also **Emotions (parental), Imitation, Happiness.**)

Permissiveness

Permissiveness is the opposite of control. Parents' permissiveness towards their child usually derives from an immediate bid for expediency and/or a specious desire always to be *liked* by the child. Permissiveness is lazy, and it is also unloving, because it denies the child the structures and boundaries she so crucially needs to contain her impulses and thus feel *safe* in her interactions with the physical world and with other people. Children of permissive parents feel insecure.

Parents who are permissive towards their children usually have an ill-formed moral code because of inadequacies in their own upbringing. They need to serve themselves and their children well by thoughtfully articulating a general philosophy of life and love to use as a reference and a guide in their loving control and discipline of their child.

(See also **Control, Discipline, Firmness, Flexibility.**)

Personality

See **Temperament.**

Pets

Most children at some time want a pet, that is a live thing of their own to play with and love, in imitation of the love their parents give them and as practice in developing their own true parenting ability.

For some children – for innate temperamental reasons, or circumstantial reasons such as being an only child – a child may deeply *need* a pet as an outlet for the nurturing and/or playful feelings that they are not presently able to bestow effectively on other people. And for some children a pet may be the means whereby they are enabled to feel that they *are* loved – by the pet – when they are transiently feeling bereft of love that has been snatched away from them by, say, bereavement or the divorce of their parents. (However, it is important that a pet be used to fulfil such a need for feeling loved only temporarily and only supplementarily to a parent's own loving efforts to heal a child's emotional wounds.)

For the sakes of both your child and the pet, make sure that your child is old enough and the pet manageable enough that he or she is able *and willing* to accept the *long-term* implications that owning a pet entails. A child is not mature enough meaningfully to look after a pet until the age of six, by which time she has developed a true basic feeling for the welfare of others as well as herself through her established moral code. If in doubt about your child's willingness and/or ability to truly care for a pet, choose a creature that is really only nominally a pet, like a tortoise. Choose a dog only for a child who has a very large impulse and ability to bestow loving care regularly, reliably, and continuously over many years.

(See also **Attachments, Birth order, Morality, Only child.**)

Phobias

A phobia is an irrational concentration of fear on a particular object or experience. A phobia may be acquired by a single experience in which fear co-existed with something intrinsically innocuous in the environment, but that innocuous thing becomes permanently tainted with the remembrance of fear. For example a child may acquire a lifelong fear of beards because her first sighting of a beard was on a dentist who hurt her.

I believe that many phobias are best left alone because they provide a useful container for a certain amount of innate fear (present in us all) which would otherwise be thinly spread over the person's general experience of life. But a phobia can be inferred to be pathological if it is of a thing or experience that a person inevitably encounters very often in everyday life. Thus, generally speaking, a mouse or spider phobia suggests a more pathological degree of fear than a fear of snakes. That is, the more underlying fear there is, the more commonplace in everyday life will be the thing or experience about which the person is phobic. (The unconscious mind is very clever indeed in the devices it chooses to express itself!)

A phobia that is a nuisance in a child's life is probably best treated by a parent's use of magic against it. *School phobia*, which occurs suddenly (as distinct from the clingingness of a child to his mother in his first days of playgroup or school) should be inferred by parents to be a manifestation of some serious dis-ease in the child, which calls for psychotherapeutic help. The most pathological phobia of all is the fear of *food*, as manifest in anorexia nervosa, which is a life-threatening dis-ease requiring prolonged and difficult psychotherapy for the deep and pervasive problems hidden beneath its phobic symptom.

(See also **Anorexia nervosa, Anxiety, Fear, Magic.**)

Playing

Playing is to children what work is to grown-ups. Playing is, for children, the chief means whereby they learn about the world, themselves in relation to the world, and themselves in relation to other people. As for grown-ups in their work, playing for children should be a hugely and happily significant part of their lives.

Never call it 'only playing', and never peremptorily interrupt a child's intense preoccupation in her play (any more than you would peremptorily interrupt a grown-up's intense preoccupation in her work). Instead, some time *before* it is time for dinner, going out, or whatever else will necessarily interrupt her play, respect her privacy and her absorption by, for example, knocking on the door of her room before entering, and saying quietly, 'Excuse me, dinner will be ready in about ten minutes, so finish off what you are doing now.'

Pocket money

See **Money.**

Possessiveness

Possessiveness is natural in human beings and should be respected in a child. Sharing is never genuine and wholehearted unless it is voluntary, and a child – like an adult – is entitled not to share what is hers if she doesn't want to. By being granted this permission a child will automatically reciprocally respect others' rights not to share their possessions with her if they don't want to. The word 'generosity' implies a degree of lovingness in a giver that transcends his or her innate self-centred possessiveness; and generosity (like lovingness in general) is paradoxically an obvious characteristic of only those people who have had their innate selfishness appropriately indulged and respected in young childhood by their parents. Children whose possessiveness is understandingly respected will automatically begin to exhibit some self-transcendent loving and sharing impulses towards others some time between three and six years of age. When such gestures occur, they should be reinforced by fulsome praise rather than taken for granted as the way the child 'ought' to be.

(See also **Jealousy, Selfishness, Sharing.**)

Potty training

Potty training is entirely unnecessary because a child's capacities to control his bowel and bladder functioning are matters of physiological – not psychological – maturation, both of which occur some time when the child is between two and three years of age.

Parents who claim to have 'trained' their child before this time have actually 'trained' themselves (as in a cartoon I once saw of some psychological laboratory pigeons, one saying to another, 'Oh boy, have I got this guy conditioned. Every time I do a trick, he drops a pellet of food into the cage')!

A couple of generations ago, in the absence of disposable nappies and washing machines, a case could be made for 'potty training', but today such 'training' creates more rather than less work for the already over-worked mother of a toddler, inasmuch as it confines her to remembering and carrying out the routine of sitting the child on the potty and waiting for it to perform. The whole issue is probably best forgotten until the child himself spontaneously indicates his readiness (by which time he is likely to be able straightaway to use the toilet and completely bypass the need for a potty).

However, bowel and bladder control is not without psychological significance for a child. Because it occurs at the one- to three-year-old stage of development, the child is very vulnerable to developing a perception that 'doing poo-poos and wee-wees on the potty or toilet' is a form of obedience to his mother's demands. Such a perception may distort the naturalness of bowel and bladder functioning into an issue of compliance or rebellion, which can become the cause of chronic disturbances, such as constipation or bedwetting. So, in the interest of avoiding such unhealthy misperceptions in the child, it is worthwhile for parents carefully to avoid 'Good girl' or 'Good boy' as forms of encouragement for using the toilet, but rather to remark, 'What a *big* girl/boy having a poo-poo/wee-wee on the toilet just like Mummy and Daddy.' In this way, bowel and bladder control is understood by the child to be a mark of his increasing *autonomy* (in which he feels pride) rather than an issue of goodness, which is a false association to these natural functions.

'Never mind' is all that needs to be said in response to an 'accident', and don't say 'Dirty'.

(See also **Bed-wetting, Constipation, Obedience, One to Three, Rebellion.**)

Prohibitions

Prohibitions test a child's obedience, and his obedience is a reminder to him of his inferior power, against which he is bound to rebel – at least sometimes – in healthy spunkiness.

A child's compliance to prohibitions can be greatly enhanced by always giving him reasons for them. This powerfully dilutes his impulse to rebellion, because he is thereby enabled to experience prohibitions other than as gratification of his parents' 'master to slave' control over him. A young child is incapable of understanding the real reasons for many prohibitions that are necessarily imposed on him, but will still deeply appreciate any 'because' that is given, however incomprehensible or spurious it is. Even those prohibitions that have to be imposed imperiously, such as 'Don't ever, ever go on the road!' are enhanced by, 'because if you do you'll get eaten up by a car'; or, 'No, you can't have another biscuit, because if you do you'll get very bad tummy ache.'

Later, from twelve to sixteen and in adolescence it is often more appropriate to say to a child, 'Because I say so' rather than to fall into the trap the child is then inclined to set you of debating with him about your prohibitions. His reasoning ability is by then as sophisticated as yours – and he may very well win in argument with you! – but you know (as he secretly does also) that the prohibitions you now insist on imposing on him are emotional or moral issues – which have nothing to do with reason.

(See also **Control, Defiance, Disobedience, Obedience, Punishment, Rebellion, Safety.**)

Protectiveness

Like the protectiveness that many other species exhibit towards their new-born young, the instinctive protectiveness that a human parent – and especially a mother – exhibits towards her new-born baby knows no bounds. This instinctive impulse is, of course, as it needs to be in the face of the total helpless vulnerability of a new-born baby.

Step by step, both physically and emotionally, helplessness gives way to competency, over the twenty or so years it takes for a human being to achieve self-sufficient maturity. The chief task of parenthood is the tightrope act – at every transitional stage of the child's development – of endorsing and encouraging the child's self-sufficiency while at the same time assuring him of the safe harbour of home and his parents' protective love when the going gets too rough for him to cope.

Being human, *all* parents are bound, from time to time, to slip off this tightrope and to err by being either under- or over-protective of their child in a specific situation. We are all rightly horrified by parents who blatantly neglect their children in allowing them pre-emptively to fend for themselves, but many people are blind to the equally horrific failure of parents who blatantly and grossly over-protect their child in the name of love. *Gross over-protectiveness is as cruel and psychologically crippling of a child as gross neglect*, in imputing and thus actually creating false helplessness in the child. A child may be under- or over-protected concerning his interactions with the physical world and/or his interactions with other people. There are parents who mollycoddle their children physically to the extent of producing hypochondria in them, while healthily encouraging them to be resilient in their relationships with other people. And there are parents who over-protect their children's feelings to the extent of denying them emotional literacy, while healthily encouraging them to shrug off the pains of their minor physical ailments and injuries.

Happily, the vast majority of parents lovingly give their children a just and right balance of protectiveness and healthy 'neglect' both physically and emotionally, and are able comfortably to accept the 'humanness' of their occasional inevitable lapses from the ideal balance. However, it is worth mentioning that for most normal, loving parents, their proneness to emotional over-protection of their child arises from their *difficulty in bearing the pain they feel in response to their child's pain*. Out of my experience as a psychotherapist, I think such parents are likely to have suffered much psychological pain in their own childhoods and so desperately want to spare their children similar suffering. But emotional as well as physical pain is inextricably a part of life itself, and parents can go a long way to healing their own wounds through bravely allowing their children to suffer sometimes – and yet resoundingly and resiliently to survive! Allow your children to suffer some bruising of their hearts as well as of their shins. We are all entitled to the fullness of life that entails pain as well as joy.

(See also **Bravery, Comforting, Independence, Worrying about your child.**)

Punishment

Contrary to popular belief, *punishment does not work in its avowed aim of eliminating undesirable behaviour.* The mistaken belief that it does work derives from the fact that, momentarily, while the punishment is actually being inflicted, it does inhibit the undesired behaviour. But behaviour that is punished will be more rather than less often expressed in the long run.

The ineffectiveness of punishment as a means of 'shaping' behaviour is far too little understood in the community at large, although animal trainers have always known it! It is incontestably proven that animals (and human beings) will more frequently express any behaviour that is *responded to* than to behaviour that is *ignored. Any* response reinforces behaviour, whether the response is rewarding *or* punitive. A rewarding response to any behaviour a child exhibits makes the child more likely to exhibit that behaviour again *and* to feel good about himself for so doing. A punitive response to any behaviour a child exhibits makes the child more likely to exhibit that behaviour again *and* to feel bad about himself for so doing. The only way to eliminate undesirable behaviour is completely and *always* to ignore it.

Now this is, of course, much easier said than done, and no parent need berate herself for failing to fulfil this ideal. However, bearing the principle in mind, and acting on it as often as possible, will enormously enhance a parent's competence in managing well to curb the unacceptable behaviour in her child. The general rule is simple: bounteously praise all behaviour in your child that you like, and ignore, as far as you possibly can, all behaviour in your child that you don't like. A harassed parent of a toddler may understandably be just so relieved at the breathing space her child has given when he goes off and plays by himself for half an hour that she keeps a safe distance from him rather than risk putting an end to the peace and quiet granted to her. However, it is very worthwhile indeed for her to go to the child and remark, '*What* a good boy you are, playing so happily by yourself.'

While it is of course impossible never to respond punitively (if only by a disapproving look), the more a parent is able – physically and psychologically – to *interestingly distract* a child from what she doesn't want him to do in favour of something else, the more generally obedient will a child be to her wishes.

The few imperious prohibitions that need to be imposed on a

child, especially from one to three years of age, such as *never* going on to the road and *never* touching the stove, need to be distinguished from punishment. They make a child feel bad by filling him with fear whenever he has an impulse to disobey, but this fear is desirable in the interests of the preservation of his life and safety. The relevant prohibitions should be imposed with sufficient threatening power that the parent can be fully confident that in these matters the child's fear will always be greater than his contrary impulses.

In the face of the recalcitrance, rudeness, dangerous and generally delinquent behaviour of teenagers, often the only effective response is the threat – followed by the actuality – of withdrawing his or her pocket money if he or she does not relent.

(See also **Control, Criticism, Discipline, Prohibitions, Temper-tantrums.**)

Quarrelling

Quarrelling is verbal fighting, and is natural and wholesome between brothers and sisters, no matter that it is also greatly distressing and exhausting to parents. An only child can be profoundly disadvantaged in not having any brothers and sisters to quarrel with, because quarrelling between brothers and sisters is actually all about learning how to make the best possible compromises between what we want for ourselves and what others want for themselves.

Shut yourself off from your children's quarrels (if necessary with the aid of earplugs). They are learning how to negotiate with their *equals* for the rest of their lives. Your interference is tantamount to their 'taking the matter to court', the resort which we would all like to avoid, and, ideally, should be able to avoid, throughout our lives.

I venture to assert that parents who never quarrel with each other are unnatural and actually have large reserves of unexpressed anger and resentment between them. Seeing their parents quarrel occasionally, and their parents' relationship nonetheless remaining essentially agreeable and loving, gives children permission themselves naturally to quarrel within nonetheless secure loving relationships. Of course children should not be witnesses to their parents' relationship being more harmful than loving. And it is crucial that *parents should never argue about their children in front of their children*.

(See also **Fighting, Selfishness.**)

Reasoning

The human mind is compartmentalized into feeling, believing and reasoning. While these compartments are, in principle, separate from each other, and may disagree with each other on any given matter, we are all most comfortable when they are in harmony within us. So when they are not in harmony, we tend to seek to make them so. Like it or not, most of our actions and choices are propelled primarily by our feelings, secondly by our beliefs, and lastly by our reasoning – which perhaps accounts for the high valuation we put on our reasoning and our 'reasonableness'. In truth, most of our reasoning is in the interests of rationalizing our feelings or justifying our beliefs, rather than being the expression of the true 'objectivity' we usually claim for it.

In rearing a child, we are overwhelmingly involved in 'believing' – that is in expressing and imposing on our child what we consider to be right and proper, rather than wrong and improper. A baby is only capable of feeling: from about one year of age, reasoning slowly develops, and believing does not even begin to develop until three to six years of age. So throughout the rearing of a child we are involved in the supportive development of the child's reasoning and believing capacities, and it is naturally appropriate that we qualify our own believing behaviour with justifying reasoning, whenever possible, in order to gain the willing compliance of the child. 'Reasoning with' a child takes more effort than simply 'laying down the law' in accordance with our beliefs, but the child is entitled to that effort on our part.

However, there are limits to the value of reasoning with a child, and 'over-reasoning' is a risk when the child is either too young to be over-burdened with it or too old to need it! *One* good reason is, by and large, sufficient for a child under six to cope with, and any continuing 'why's' beyond that are best dealt with by 'I've explained why.' From twelve to sixteen and in adolescence, argumentative reasoning is often a deliberate ploy on the part of the child to evade acknowledging the demands of morality and responsibilities, which are functions of believing, and quite independent of reasoning. It behoves parents to see through this ploy and firmly resist it, if necessary with, 'Because I say so.'

(See also **Conformity, Morality, Obedience, Prohibitions, Responsibilities.**)

Rebellion

Rebellion is the obverse of obedience. Any child who is *never* rebellious, 'naughty', or disobedient towards his parents and other authorities is pathologically repressed, and will pay the price sooner or later, of serious anxiety and psychological disfunctioning in his or her adult life.

Obedience versus rebellion is a central issue in a child's natural development between one and three and twelve and sixteen years of age. From one to three, notwithstanding the many impulses the child expresses that need to be controlled, at core he generally wants to be and is obedient to his parents. From twelve to sixteen, at the core of his being the child is – and needs to be – generally rebellious towards his parents. Out of his symmetrical experiences of being obedient (from one to three) and rebellious (from twelve to sixteen), the child is enabled maturely to express appropriate degrees of both compliance and dominant authority in his grown-up intimate relationships and in his interpersonal transactions in the world at large.

(See also **Control, Defiance, Discipline, Disobedience, Obedience.**)

Regression

Each stage of development along the path from birth to maturity is based on the accumulated achievements of every previous stage of development. We can't learn to run before we can walk. And, as we embark on each new stage of development and struggle to achieve new competences, we have an inbuilt defensive mechanism that prompts us to retreat to already established competences in a bid to salve our hurt pride when the going gets rough.

When we fall too often in our attempts to run, we content ourselves with walking; when we fall too often in our attempts to walk, we content ourselves with crawling. Returning to more immature forms of behaviour when we find ourselves unable to meet present challenges is called 'regression in the service of the ego'. It occurs at least as often in our emotional struggles as our physical ones, and can be observed in response to severely testing episodes in our grown-up lives as well as in childhood.

In early childhood, especially between the ages of about two and four, obviously regressive behaviour (such as baby-talk, thumb-sucking and crawling) is very common in response to the stresses the toddler is experiencing in learning a huge array of new physical skills and taking huge strides in his psychological independence. So I think that regressive behaviour in a pre-school age child is best neither corrected nor endorsed, but rather tolerated although largely ignored.

When at any age a child's current competence is obviously over-stretched by some particular circumstance, such as house-moving or the birth of a new baby, read the regressive behaviour as a sign that all is not well with the child, and do your best to discover and dissolve the underlying cause of his distress.

(See also **Anorexia nervosa, Independence, Responsibilities.**)

Rejection

Rejection is the obverse of intimacy. Close, loving family intimacy is the fundamental basis that enables a child to become a generally happy and wholesome grown-up and, particularly, to be able to form a loving, intimate family life of his own.

However, in order for a grown-up child healthily to form a new family of his own, he has to disengage from the family created by his parents, and this process begins with the vehement rebellion of puberty, and is consolidated in later adolescence by a degree of *cold, rejecting detachment* the child exudes towards his or her parents. The child's rejection is directed more pointedly to his or her opposite-sexed parent than to his or her same-sexed parent. This is because sexual impulses now very explicitly contaminate his feelings of loving intimacy (towards anybody), and so he or she is (naturally and healthily) very uncomfortable in relating intimately to his or her opposite-sexed parent. While the opposite-sexed parent is more maturely capable than the child of separating his or her affectionate and sexual impulses, the parent, too, is often uncomfortably aware of the child as a sexual being, and is glad of the increasing distance between them.

Wise and loving parents appreciate the wholesome naturalness of their child's need to reject them in adolescence. It is healthy for them reciprocally (but without the child's over-stated hostility) also to reject the child, especially by looking forward – and letting the child know they are looking forward – to the time when they, Mother and Father, freed of parental responsibilities, will enjoy renewed greater intimacy with each other.

When parents and child thus healthily detach from each other, the child will go out into the world and find a committed sexual relationship of his own. With his rivalry towards his same-sexed parent and his incestuous impulses towards his opposite-sexed parent no longer issues, he will resume a non-sexual, non-competitive, simply loving relationship with both his parents.

(See also **Incest, Intimacy, Love, Rivalry, Separation.**)

Religion

See **God.**

Responsibilities

Being responsible in general is a permission acquired by a child through the example of his or her parents. Particular responsibilities accepted by the child increase – from birth to maturity – in parallel with the child's increasing autonomy and associated privileges.

As a rule of thumb I think it is probably best to ask a child to accept a new responsibility (and associated privilege) only when he is somewhat *more than ready* to do so. In every aspect of learning – in grown-ups as well as children – we all tend to moments of pre-emptive excitement and confidence before our learning is fully consolidated. I remember, for example, my own desire to drive through the centre of London before my driving teacher judged I was ready to do so. His insistence on my being patient increased my eagerness, kept me safe, and gave me the final reward of driving confidently and well – without hiccups – when he finally gave me the permission I was then capable of.

If a child accepts a responsibility before he is fully capable – physically or psychologically – of maintaining it continuously, his self-esteem is likely to be damaged every time he 'forgets', and his overall attitude to responsibilities in general will tend to be half-hearted. Ask a child to be fully responsible, from now on, for cleaning his own teeth, walking to school on his own, making his own bed, earning his pocket money by cleaning the car each week, etc. only when he is well and truly old enough to do so. Then he will maintain his responsibilities with ease and pride, and will willingly accept and carry out his responsibilities in grown-up life.

(See also **Birth order, Guilt, Independence, Regression.**)

Righteousness

The quest for righteousness is intrinsic to human nature, but it is also that attribute which spoils the happiness of interpersonal relationships more than anything else. If we reflect honestly on what is actually happening in all the quarrels and upsets that occur between us and other people, it all boils down to each party insisting on his or her own 'rightness' and wanting the other party to admit their 'wrongness'.

As soon as a clear sense of 'self' develops in a child – as evidenced by her use of the word 'I' – from about two years of age, her quest for righteousness begins as the necessary defence against her fear of (and presumption of) abandonment or some lesser form of withdrawal of love or punishment if she is 'bad' or 'wrong'. Unless we are very wise – perhaps 'saintly' – we never, at any time in our lives, completely transcend our quests for righteousness, although, in the normal course of our grown-up lives, as our self-confidence becomes increasingly assured, we are increasingly able to say and to mean, 'I'm sorry, I was wrong. Please forgive me.' (There is nothing so conducive to love between people as their capacity and willingness to say this.)

A young child is only able to defend her need for righteousness very crudely, by *denial*, which is often so blatant as to be amusing to grown-ups, whose defences are so much more sophisticated. Thus my two-year-old grand-daughter dropped and broke a plate in full view of me and simply said, 'I didn't do it.' But at three she was beginning to have an inkling that she could defend her righteousness more potently by *blaming* somebody else (which, in subtle ways, is what grown-ups do all the time). So, at three, when she was sitting opposite me at the supper table and accidently dropped some food on the floor, she looked me straight in the eye and said, 'I think you did that'!

Accept your child's needs to defend her righteousness as a natural human characteristic. While there is no need to endorse it, it is cruelly unjustified to accuse the child of lying in her first crude attempts to defend her righteousness. Furthermore, such punishment only reinforces the child's felt need to 'defend' herself with even greater tenacity in the future. Much better, in response to an accidentally broken plate and 'I didn't' or 'You did it', is a nonchalant response of, 'Never mind, it was an accident. Let's pick up the pieces and throw them in the rubbish bin.' Thus, by your non-punitive response, the child is assured that you have *not* withdrawn your love because she has done something wrong, so her fear of reprisal and her associated defensive righteousnesses are both diminished. Parents who, in this way, sensitively diminish their young child's *need* to be righteous are bestowing on her a very great gift indeed.

(See also **Apologizing, Good and evil, Guilt.**)

Rivalry

Rivalry is a combination of competitiveness and jealousy. Its archetypal manifestation occurs first in the Oedipal stage of development, from three to six years of age, when the child becomes competitive towards the same-sexed parent out of his or her jealousy of the love given by his or her opposite-sexed parent to his or her same-sexed parent. This archetypal theme of rivalry is reiterated in adolescence, which prepares the child for final emotional-sexual detachment from his or her parents in favour of forming an emotional-sexual attachment of his or her own.

Derivatively, there is natural rivalry between brothers and sisters for the love of both their parents. Further derivatives are found in currying favour with teachers and, in adult life, with sexual rivals and with bosses at work. Without the natural experience of rivalry in our early family lives, we grow up with a grandiose presumption of our entitlement to have all our wishes immediately granted by others. With *too much* experience of rivalry in our early family lives, we grow up to have a self-deprecating expectation that others will always claim and get what we want, instead of us. It is a difficult but important task of parenting to do our best to make each of our children balanced in their expectations of 'giving' and 'getting' in all their interactions with others. The pattern of attitudes and behaviour learnt by the child in the triangular relationship between him- or herself and his or her parents from three to six years of age will tend to be reiterated in all analogous situations throughout his or her life.

(See also **Competitiveness, Envy, Jealousy, Sexuality, Three to six.**)

Routine

All human beings, throughout their lives, seek a happy balance of safe certainty and exciting uncertainty. Routine provides the predictable structures that serve our need for safe certainty, and children, in their tender vulnerabilities, need more routine than most grown-ups do. Children who are given too little predictable routine in their daily lives grow up to be very nervous, restless, and insecure in their relationships both to the physical world and to other people. On the other hand, too unwavering a routine in a child's life produces an obsessively rigid grown-up whose capacity for spontaneity, adventurousness, and general risk-taking is miserably restricted. A happy balance between routine and unpredictability is the ideal for all of us.

Parents usually become aware of the need to balance routine and spontaneity from the earliest weeks and months of their baby's life. At this early stage it is more in the interest of her own wellbeing than that of the child that a mother typically struggles to establish some predictability in the baby's eating and sleeping patterns, while also retaining some flexibility in her responses to his demands. But even at this stage of his life, a baby's – as well as his mother's – overall wellbeing will be enhanced rather than diminished by her insistence, for example, that he goes to sleep when *she* knows he is tired, not withstanding his vociferous disagreement.

When in doubt err in favour of routine, as its excess is less damaging to a child in the long-run than an equivalent excess of uncertainty. Stable routines around going to bed, cleaning teeth, washing hands after going to the toilet, eating meals calmly and regularly, are especially important because they are associated with basic bodily welfare and, at a sub-conscious level, assure the child that he is 'looked after'. As these routines become the child's own 'second nature', he experiences himself as confidently always looking after his bodily welfare. Thus, with his deeply assured sense of routine in those matters that keep him deeply *safe*, he can look for and enjoy adventures of unpredictability in the rest of his life. I believe this truth applies equally to intellectual structures in life. Thus I am a firm believer in schooling incorporating a fair amount of rigid structure – learning tables, grammar, spelling, etc. – as the necessary foundation without which 'creative self-expression' is an inauthentic camouflage for deeply disconcerting chaos in the child's perceptions.

(See also **Flexibility, Safety, Security.**)

Safety

Safety versus adventurousness is the 'bottom line' duality of impulse in all our lives. Fear can prompt us to excessive safety measures that stultify us and take all the spontaneity out of our lives. Curiosity and adventurousness can prompt us to excessive risk-taking that may make us accident-prone and generally self-destructive. Consciously or unconsciously, all our important decision-making involves the struggle to find the just-right balance between safety and adventure in our lives.

By and large, children under the age of about three, and between the ages of twelve and sixteen, are inclined to excessive risk-taking, which needs to be counteracted by parents' prohibitiveness. By and large, children between the ages of six and twelve are inclined to excessive fearfulness, which needs to be counteracted by parents' enthusiastic encouragement.

(See also **Prohibitions, Protectiveness, Routine, Worrying about your child.**)

School

A child's starting school marks a profoundly important turning point in a child's life as he begins to form significant attachments to people outside the family and begins to have to fend for himself, away from his mother. A child's starting school is usually also a significant and poignant moment for parents as they become fully conscious that healthy parenting means letting go of *their* dependence on their child's dependence on them.

(See also **Independence, Protectiveness, Teachers.**)

Security

So long as he is not abandoned, the basic security of a child under the age of about five is vouchsafed by his belief in the God-like omniscience and omnipotence of his parents. Mummy and Daddy 'know everything' and are capable of making everything all right, no matter what the difficulties. From about five onwards, Mummy and Daddy have to compete with other authorities – especially teachers – for 'rightness' in matters of fact and opinion, but the child's *emotional* security goes on depending on his ability to perceive his parents as unambiguously powerful in their capacity to keep him safe and sound. And even when he is grown-up, as long as his parents are alive, a child is entitled to perceive his parents as always available, when the going gets rough, for the unconditional loving support that they alone are uniquely *always* willing to give him.

The relationship between parents and children is not symmetrical, and *parents do not have the right to reciprocal support for their emotional (or material) security from their children.* Parents who fully love their children will be loved by them in return, and the children will spontaneously and willingly do all they can to be a nurturing presence in their parents' lives as their parents age. But this is not an *entitlement* of the parents as the child's nurturance by his parents in his entitlement for the whole of his parents' lives.

From this it follows that parents should never, if at all possible – and certainly never before the child is fully grown-up – burden their child with their own emotional problems. They must seek elsewhere for parental-type nourishment when they need it. Each generation has non-reciprocal obligations to the generation that comes after it, and the fulfilment of these obligations is its own reward in the feeling of 'life well-lived' that is the outcome.

Most particularly, parents must never be '*hurt by*' their children. Parents are the natural sounding board against which children bounce off all their developing emotions, and they need and are entitled to express hostile and rejecting as well as warm and loving feelings towards their parents in the course of their maturation, without the consequence of sick guilt imposed on them by parents saying, 'After all we've done for you . . .', etc.

(See also **Control, Emotions (parental), God, Guilt, Hate, Insecurity, Love, Permissiveness.**)

Selfishness

To angrily accuse a child – or grown-up – of 'selfishness' is an act of thoughtless hypocrisy because, in truth, both materially and emotionally, we are all selfish. It is much more honest to teach our children that everybody is naturally selfish but that we all, ultimately, get *more* of what we want from others if we sometimes give them what they want in advance of demanding what we want.

(See also **Love, Manners, Possessiveness, Quarrelling, Sharing.**)

Separation

Although a baby, very soon after birth, comes to recognize the smell, sound, sight, touch, and taste of his mother as the most gratifying presence in his universe, it is not until he is about seven months old that he becomes aware that his *survival* depends on her. So long as a baby under the age of about seven months receives plenty of tender, loving care – including plenty of physical touching, which is the essential *psychological* nourishment he needs at this stage – a mother may leave her baby in the loving care of another adult while she takes some time off to 'be herself', without any adverse psychological repercussions in her baby.

But from about seven months onwards, a baby's separation from his mother produces extreme *panic* in him, and his lifelong psychological well-being depends on such episodes being kept to a minimum until he is about two years old, by which time he is capable of understanding and accepting, with some equanimity, that 'Mummy is going shopping, but will be back soon.' To the extent that a mother is bound to leave her child from time to time, it is less traumatizing for him – before he is about two – for her to disappear while he is not noticing her, rather than saying 'Bye bye', which instigates the panic in him that may otherwise be avoided. However, I believe that the separation of a mother from her under-six-year-old child should always be a matter of hours at the most, never days unless absolutely unavoidable. I have seen lifelong deep-seated personality disorders of fearful insecurity induced by no more than a few days' necessary hospitalization of a child (when his mother was not domiciled in the hospital with him).

On return from a separation, it is important for parents to cope with the symptoms of the child's inevitable traumatization, which may include (defensive) turning away from them as well as fear and clingingness, for even up to several weeks. A loving mother, recognizing the critical importance of healing the child's wound *now* rather than letting it get 'covered over' with lifelong maladaptive 'defences', will accept the need for a prolonged period of extra-close reassuringness towards her child.

Very gradually, over the whole of a child's development to maturity, he becomes capable of tolerating increasing spans of time in which he is separated from his mother. But even in adolescence – notwithstanding his dismissive contrary avowals – a child still feels somewhat abandoned if he comes home from school to an empty house. He is still deeply comforted by the smells, sounds, sights, touches, and tastes associated with the haven of home, when his mother is there to welcome him. When the final healthy separation from the parents takes place in late adolescence, it should always be the child, not the parents, who instigate it.

(See also **Child care, Hospitalization, Working mothers.**)

Sex instruction

There seems to be a natural reticence between most parents and their own children in talking to each other about the actualities of sex. Despite this, parents must, of course, answer their children's questions honestly, if reservedly, and make appropriate books freely accessible to their children.

I believe that basic instruction about 'the facts of life' is best given at school by teachers who are not entangled emotionally with the children they teach as the children's parents are. And this basic instruction is best given in primary school, at which stage in their development children are most able to accept such instruction matter-of-factly.

Generally speaking, parents *and* their children are relieved to *not* have to talk about sex to each other – which I believe is healthy. Indeed, I think parents who argue the case for 'total uninhibited honesty' in talking to their children about sex should question their own motives in so doing. Certainly from puberty onwards, no father should talk to his daughter and no mother should talk to her son about the explicit actualities of sexual behaviour.

(See also **Custody, Incest, Modesty, Sexuality, Step-children.**)

Sexism

In my opinion, the assumption that stereotypical gender distinctions in attitudes and behaviour are wholly conditioned is false. There is a great deal of evidence that, collectively speaking, there are many biologically determined differences between girls and boys that inform an equal number of corresponding psychological differences between the sexes. I believe that, on average, girls *are* more interested in dolls and people and feelings; and boys more interested in cars and things and facts. Girls *are* more receptive; boys more aggressive.

None of this denies that in his or her individuality any particular girl or boy may diverge from average in her or his gender-linked characteristics. And, of course, such individualistic divergence from average should be respected and endorsed. But, by and large, encouraging girls to be 'feminine' and boys to be 'masculine' inculcates the enormously valuable attributes in a child of clear gender identity and sexual self-esteem.

There are no communities on earth that do not pointedly distinguish the sexes in terms of expected psychological attitudes and roles in life as well as in terms of anatomy and physiology, no matter how different any other culture's specific stereotyping may be from our own.

Vive la difference!

(See also **Homosexuality, Sexuality.**)

Sexuality

Sexuality, together with aggression, constitutes the energetic life force in us all. Most basically, sexuality is the impulse for *skin contact* with other human beings and, at this level, is a vital need in infancy, when our very survival depends on it. Gradually, this simple need gives way to differentiated sexual impulses and increasing discrimination in our choice of object for our sexual desires. This continues until, all being well, at puberty, we become committed, physically, to genital contact with members of the opposite sex and, a few years later, we become committed, emotionally, to the 'type' of man or woman who psychologically embodies our personal mythic dream of love.

While a case can be made for some people having an innate pre-

disposition to a homosexual orientation throughout life, by and large
the evidence is overwhelming that an individual's lifelong adult
sexual propensities are *made* through his or her contingent familial
experiences from three to six years of age.

In broad terms, human sexuality progresses from self-love up
until the age of three; a flirtatious bid for the preferential love of the
opposite-sexed parent from three to six; a withdrawal into 'latency',
manifest as a preference for essentially asexual friendships with
same-sexed peers from six to twelve; a confused homo-heterosexual
genital orientation from twelve to sixteen, which gives way, in later
adolescence, to a full, unambiguous heterosexual genital orientation. Each new developmental stage incorporates the learning
of the stages that have preceded it. We never 'outgrow' – in sexual
or any other matters – our commitment to what we learned at earlier
stages of our development. Rather what we learn at each stage 'con-
taminates' subsequent stages by narrowing the possibilities of our
future perceptions.

Our completed selves are like towers of blocks, with each block
depending for its stability and orientation on the one on which it
rests, which, in turn, depends on the one on which it rests . . . to the
base block of our very earliest infantile experiences. The 'colour' of
each 'block of development' for each person may be any of the
whole spectrum, and the shape of each block may be very varied.
Nobody's tower is ever completely harmonious in colour or smooth
in outline, or so stable as to be invulnerable to knocks. When we are
knocked, a number of our blocks will fall off the top of our tower to
reveal an ill-shaped or badly laid block underneath, which needs to
be adjusted before we can build ourselves up again to our full
stature, with increased stability, invulnerability, and confidence.
And because our sexuality pervades the whole of our being and
doing in the world, it is primarily through our sexual relationships
with other people, and secondly through our relationships with
other people in general, that we all inevitably spend our lives
adjusting and re-orienting the 'towers' of our being.

Thus it follows that what a child explicitly and implicitly learns
from his or her parents about sexuality in the whole course of his
development to maturity will be a profound influence on his experiences for the rest of his life. As parents, being human, we cannot –
and nor should we ask of ourselves – that we do a 'perfect' job.
However, there are some general principles which, used as
guidelines by loving parents, will ensure that their child grows up to

have an essentially happy and wholesome attitude to sex and – derivatively – to life in general.

1 As a child gradually begins to know, factually, what sexual intercourse actually *is*, he is appalled and revulsed by the idea of his parents 'doing it'. The origin and meaning of this revulsion is open to question, but it may be inferred that, principally, it serves the primary, universal *incest taboo*. But whatever its meaning, knowledge of his parents as sexual beings is extremely discomfiting to a child, and his being an actual witness to explicit sexual behaviour between them is extremely *traumatizing to him for the rest of his life*. The child is entitled never to have this experience imposed on him nor to *hear about* what happens sexually between his parents or (in the case of divorced parents) what happens to either of them sexually with other partners.

2 Sex is a moral matter, and children need to be explicitly *taught* this by their parents, because, at face value, the idea of 'hurting somebody else' by the fulfilment of mutual desire doesn't make sense. Particularly in adolescence, it behoves parents insistently to impose on the child their exhortations that he or she just *has to* accept the parents' knowledge – which the child simply doesn't have – that sexual intercourse before maturity – say eighteen – is bound to be, for the child and his or her partner – an extremely *damaging* experience, no matter how much 'in love' the child feels him- or herself to be.

While reasoning is beside the point, I think it does have value to an adolescent to have explained that, before full maturity is reached, the deep damage that can be done to his or her long-term well-being through the premature experience of full sexual intercourse derives from the deep misunderstanding between teenage girls and boys. A teenage boy is overwhelmed by the imperious and indiscriminate demands of his hormones for sexual release, but he is quite removed from any concept which necessarily unites sex and love. A teenage girl is overwhelmed by her desire for romance, but her capacity to cope physically or psychologically with the furore of sexual passion is still ill-formed. Only by about twenty are boys *beginning* to think of love, and girls *beginning* to be sexually orgasmic. Before then a girl needs to be taught her responsibility implicitly to teach boys about love by resisting their lustful advances. Before then a boy needs to be taught his responsibility to respect the profound emotional vulnerability of girls to the act of sex, which vulnerability he does not share.

Many adolescents will, of course, defy the sexual – as well as many other – moral imperatives imposed on them by their parents. But if and when they break the sexual rules and are in some way made unhappy by so doing, the *happy ideal* proposed to them by their parents is still available to them for future hope. The sexually permissive parents of recent generations of adolescents are answerable for the many young adults whose attitude to sex has been nothing more than 'an appetite to be appeased', having become – even in their early twenties – sadly despairing of there being anything in life worth living for.

3 From about the age of three onwards, a child is fully aware of gender distinctions and so becomes fully vulnerable to any unhealthy sexual nuances between himself or herself and his or her opposite-sexed parent. It is imperative from three onwards that the child *never* gets the impression that his or her opposite-sexed parent loves him or her more than that parent loves his or her same-sexed parent. So, from age three onwards, if, for any reason, a child is taken into his parents' bed, it is my opinion that he should not be allowed to lie between them: a boy should always lie on the side of the bed next to his father, a girl next to her mother. A single parent should *never* share his or her bed with an opposite-sexed child.

4 A child's sexual curiosity begins with curiosity about his or her own and other people's 'bottoms', including touching, which is natural, although appropriately discouraged except in privacy. The more a parent matter-of-factly makes modesty a matter of good manners and accepts the naturalness of even a very young child's masturbatory impulses, the more wholesomely straightforward will be the child's lifelong attitude to his or her sexuality. Punishment for *any* curiosity – even by a look of mild disapproval – reinforces rather than diminishes a child's interest and, if applied to his sexual interest, will taint the wholesomeness of his sexuality with unnecessary and neurotic guilt.

5 Parents, as well as their children, are naturally inhibited about talking to each other about 'the facts of life'. While it is appropriate for parents always to respond honestly to the child's spontaneous questions about sex with the *simplest possible* answers, by and large the acquisition of knowledge of the physiology and anatomy of sex can be confidently left to teachers and 'nature'. What is uniquely the parents' responsibility is to give their child a lifelong permission to experience sex as contained within a committed and loving relationship, as demonstrated by their relationship to each other. It is

natural for parents as well as children sometimes to quarrel and, indeed, it is probably more wholesome for a child to know this reality rather than be protected from it. But what he also needs to witness is the warmth and affectionate 'making up' of his parents as well, which assures him of their abiding love for each other. *The quality of the parents' relationship to each other is overwhelmingly the most significant determiner of the quality of the sexual-emotional relationships the child will experience throughout his or her life.*

(See also **Custody, Homosexuality, Incest, Intimacy, Love, Manners, Masturbation, Modesty, Morality, Sex instruction, Sexism.**)

Sharing

Sharing what we have with another goes against the grain of the essential selfishness in all human beings. 'It's mine!' should not be abhorred in a child – or a grown-up! – because it manifests a healthy recognition of property rights and implies knowledge that others have the right not to share *their* things also. But socialization rightly demands that we sometimes transcend our basic selfishness. Paradoxically, it is the child whose 'It's mine!' is respected who will, in due course (from about age four onwards), spontaneously and lovingly give to others.

Fundamentally, we are only willing to share what we have with another, today, in order that, reciprocally, the other will be willing to share with us what he has, tomorrow. On each occasion when sharing is necessary or appropriate, make the underlying principle *fairness*. A good trick when a piece of chocolate cake has to be shared between two is to give one child the right to cut the cake and the other the right to choose which piece to have!

(See also **Generosity, Manners, Possessiveness.**)

Shyness

Shyness has two sides: modesty and self-centredness. The opposite of shyness is arrogance, which also has two sides: self-confidence and insensitivity. A shy child needs to be encouraged to maintain the sweet sensitivity of her modesty while surrendering her self-centredness in favour of self-confidence.

Self-confidence is the opposite of self-centredness. The interest we have in the world and in other people is fuelled by the energy we have *left over* after we have looked after our own needs. Self-confident people know themselves and accept themselves, and so have plenty of energy left over for thinking about things and people other than themselves. Self-centred people use all their energy up in struggling to 'create the right impression' on other people because they do not accept themselves. Self-confident people are usually charming people: self-centred people are usually 'a pain in the neck'.

Make your child think well of himself by your abundant, explicitly given, loving approval of him, and he will not be shy.

(See also **Handicaps, Loneliness, Timidity.**)

Single parent

The most important awareness that a single parent needs to have in her relationship to her child is that the child is inclined to the un-wholesome attitude that he or she has to 'look after Mummy'. From puberty onwards, a single mother needs to make explicit to her child that she is very much looking forward to him or her leaving home, at which time she will start a new and happily more selfish life, freed from the responsibility of daily parenting (even if this is not particularly how she feels). Any indication that a child pities the parent her single status should be firmly rebuked, and the child told, with confidence and vehemence, that she, the parent, is presently very content with her status, that if and when she wants a husband, she will get one – and it is none of the child's business, anyway!

In the case of the single mother of a son (or a single father of a daughter), the rejection of the child by the parent has to be even more heavily underlined than it needs to be between a single parent and her or his same-sexed child. Especially when the child is from three to six years old, and from puberty onwards, the opposite-sexed child of a single parent needs either to have an explicit sexual rival for his mother's love or, if his mother is unattached, to have almost daily contact with a man who is willing to be an *authoritative* male role model for the child. In adolescence, boarding school may be the best option for the son of a single mother or the daughter of a single father.

(See also **Custody, Divorce, Independence, Rejection.**)

Sleep problems

Once a child is about two years old (and has all his teeth), sleep problems are typically about the child refusing to go to bed early enough at night, waking up in the middle of the night and wanting to sleep in his parents' bed, or insisting on getting up too early in the morning for his parents' comfort.

A child knows that his parents are glad to have some peace and quiet away from him in the evenings, and he seeks to sabotage them in this aim. Often he is curious about what they are doing in his absence, or else decides to test their ability to control him. He may have temper tantrums about going to bed and/or may reappear (either with manipulative cuteness or in a state of distress, claiming he has had a nightmare or something else) after his parents believe him to be soundly asleep for the night. Particularly from three to six, at which stage he is very jealous of his parents' exclusive intimacy with each other, he is likely manipulatively to disturb their privacy (which is more or less limited to the evenings, when he is supposed to be asleep).

Whether it is about going to bed or reappearing in the living room later, the issue needs *consistently* to be dealt with by firm control, in which case it is unlikely to occur more than a very few times. If the child pleads that he is 'not tired', give him explicit permission to stay awake and read or play *in bed*, but the time that he goes to bed should be part of the only very rarely varied routine in his life. When he gets out of bed and makes his reappearance in the living room he should immediately and firmly – but without anger – simply be taken straight back, without allowing him any evasive cuteness or conversation.

For any child over the age of two, waking up in the middle of the night and wanting to come into the parents' bed is an extension of wanting to be with the parents in the evening before they have gone to bed. Of course a child is entitled to be comforted when he has a nightmare and wakes up frightened, or has tummy ache; but he needs to be comforted while in his own bed and – except *in extremis* – *have no expectation that his parents will take him into bed with them*. On those (very rare) occasions when the child is greatly distressed or in pain and a parent is him- or herself so desperately tired as to resort to the expediency of taking the child into the parents' bed, after a few minutes or (if the parent meanwhile goes to sleep) when the parent next turns over and is reminded of the child's presence, he or she should carry the child back to his or her own bed, without comment if the child is asleep or, if the child is awake, saying, 'It's time to go back to your own bed now.' Letting a child sleep in his parents' bed until they get up in the morning invokes in the child a habit of expectation that, with just a little manipulativeness, he can achieve this privilege – to which he is *not* entitled, on a regular basis. This is an initial act of expediency on the part of the parents that costs them dearly. Deconditioning of this – or any other– bad habit is probably best achieved by bribery.

From one to three years of age, a child is often beset by various fears – usually derivative from the fear of abandonment – on being left to go to sleep by himself. While it can be extremely irritating to a tired parent, longing for a bit of relaxation, to sit by the bedside of her child while he goes to sleep, I think the child is entitled to this reassurance at this stage of his development. However, almost inevitably, he will go on demanding that his mother stay with him even when he has outgrown his fearfulness of going to sleep on his own, and a parent needs to wean her child firmly from this. A way of doing this is to say to the child, 'I'm going to sit with you for ten minutes, then I'm going downstairs to read my book' and if, at the end of ten minutes the child is still awake, kiss him goodnight and say, 'I'm going downstairs to read my book now' – and go straightaway without giving the child the right of reply!

When a young child wakes up in the mornings long before his parents want to, it simply has to be accepted that this is normal and typical for most young children (as lying in bed till lunchtime or beyond is normal and typical for most adolescents, if they are given the chance). From about three years old onwards, though, a glass of orange juice and a biscuit near the child's bed may grant the parents half an hour's extra sleep. Gradually the child needs to understand that Mummy and Daddy get up at 7 o'clock (or whenever), and before that, if he is awake, he must play contentedly by himself.

(See also **Abandonment, Bribery, Control, Fear, Firmness, Habits, Routine, Temper-tantrums, Wakefulness**.)

Sleepwalking

When we are asleep we are far from inactive. Our bodies move a great deal in the course of a night's sleep, and our brains seethe with the activity of our dreams. Our sub-conscious motivations dominate us during the third of our lives we spend in sleep, and the fantastic nature of our dreams gives us some access to the deepest levels of our unconscious minds, which are totally inaccessible and foreign to our waking, conscious selves.

Notwithstanding all the movement of our bodies and minds while we are asleep, sleepwalking is *abnormal*. Whatever it is the person does while sleepwalking, it must be inferred to be something he *wants* to do, even though it may be totally contrary to the wishes of his *conscious* mind. Indeed, what he does when sleepwalking is likely to be abhorrent to his conscious, waking mind – something he is only able to do under the camouflage of the 'can't help it' of sleep. Thus it must be inferred that the sleepwalker is suffering some deep dis-ease of his psyche, and psychotherapeutic help should be sought to uncover this dis-ease and cure it.

Smacking

While often used and defended by parents as the most expedient means of disciplining a child, psychologically and physically, smacking has the same quality as battering. It is a humiliating assault by a powerful person against a powerless one. It is a form of expediency that only succeeds in controlling the child's behaviour for a very short time. It instils a 'might is right' assumption in the child, and is entirely unnecessary and – except momentarily – ineffective as a means of controlling or disciplining the child.

(See also **Control, Discipline, Punishment.**)

Smoking

See **Addiction.**

Sociability

Human beings are innately sociable, and recent experiments with babies only a few days old show that they are more responsive to any human face (or a representation of a human face) than to any other stimulus.

However, it is not until a child is about three years of age that she begins to be capable of real *reciprocity* in her interactions with other people. Under the age of three, 'other people' are distinguished from each other essentially in terms of whether they fulfil or frustrate the child's impulses and desires.

Between the ages of three and six, children become capable of true *caring and sharing* in their relationships to other people.

Between the ages of six to twelve, the sexes typically separate from each other, girls preferring friendships with other girls, boys preferring friendships with other boys. By this means the child consolidates his or her *gender identity* and also learns how, sometimes, to subsume his or her individual identity in the interest of *'team spirit'*.

From puberty onwards, sociability becomes predominantly *sexually motivated* (although same-sexed friendships continue to be formed on the basis of *like-to-likeness* between people).

The essentially asexual friendships children form between the ages of about six and twelve are a necessary precursor to their ability, later, to form satisfactory friendships with the opposite sex.

(See also **Attachments, Companions, Friends, Intimacy, Loneliness, Shyness, Talking to strangers.**)

Spacing of children

Psychologically, the ideal age difference between a child and his or her next-born brother or sister is three to six years, because from three to six a child is naturally developing his capacity for *nurturing* (and ultimately *parenting*) love, so a new baby will be welcomed by the older child as an appropriate object on which to practise these developing skills.

The biggest barrier to a child under the age of three easily accepting a new baby in the family is that he is not yet old enough to be willing or able to share (except under extreme sufferance), and when there is a new baby he is called on to share – and very generously! – the most precious thing in the world to him, his mother's loving attention. So it is incumbent on the mother of a child under three *and* a baby to be sensitive to the reality, in the early months of the baby's life, that the elder child needs and is entitled to as much tender compensation for his jealousy as his mother can possibly manage. Do not ask a child under three to admire or even notice the new baby; he notices quite enough, and his natural feelings for the baby are aggressive hostility and jealous rage. Understand and give him permission to feel these natural feelings, and be content if you succeed in getting him just to leave the baby alone.

While it is inappropriate to demand of a child under three that he expresses tenderness or be willing to share anything with another child – or anybody else! – it is equally necessary to a child's healthy development that between three and six his naturally burgeoning capacities for love and sharing be reinforced by putting him into situations where these qualities are demanded of him. A younger brother or sister provides such a situation ideally. Inasmuch as every family inevitably has a youngest child who cannot have the benefit of a younger sibling, a child who, from three to six, does not have a younger brother or sister is in need of a pet of some kind on which to lavish loving tenderness.

(See also **Birth order, Jealousy, Only child, Pets, Sharing.**)

Speech.

See **Baby-talk, Language.**

Spoiling

Spoiling a child is not, as many people think, simply a matter of 'over-indulgence'. It is rather *giving a child what the parents (or others) presume he or she wants, without the child ever having to ask.* Such children grow up seriously incapacitated in their ability to know what they want, and with a chronic *manipulativeness* towards other people (which is actually a recapitulation of their relationship to their parents with everybody else), including a presumption that other people *should* read their minds and give them what they want without they themselves ever explicitly *asking*. Such grown-ups are automatically evasive and devious in all their transactions with others, and are extremely handicapped in their ability to relate to others on an equal to equal basis, or to relate with wholehearted passion and commitment in an intimate sexual relationship.

Typically, a man who was a spoilt child will be deeply unwilling to take the initiative in wooing and winning a woman; instead he will manipulate the woman into initiating the relationship and controlling him in it, in response to which he will express a mixture of clinging dependency and hostile resentment. A woman who was a spoilt child will similarly be both clingingly dependent and hostile in her intimate relationships, and she will be inclined only to relate to men who are willing to be continuously materially indulgent of her. Both men and women who are 'spoilt' are profoundly crippled by their reduction of intimacy to 'appearances', and their inability to know themselves or others with any depth of understanding or feeling.

The antithesis of spoiling a child is giving him or her permission to know what she feels and wants, to accept responsibility for communicating what she feels for and wants from others, and to respect the autonomous right of others to comply with or refuse her requests. A spoilt child is usually one who has also been made to be too obedient, which is the other face of the *lack of autonomy and responsibility*, which is the hallmark of being spoilt.

(See also **Independence, Rejection.**)

Stammering/stuttering

Stammering or stuttering is almost always a *symptom* of tense nervousness or anxiety; only very rarely is it the result of a physical speech impediment.

Between the ages of about two to four, as a child's language skills are developing very rapidly indeed, stammering or stuttering is commonplace and obviously associated with the child's struggles to find the appropriate words with which to express his thoughts.

If stammering or stuttering in a child continues chronically beyond the age of about five, in the absence of any physical impediment, assume that it is the symptom of some dis-ease in the child. Discover the underlying meaning of the child's nervousness – if necessary with the help of a psychotherapist – and the stammering or stuttering will almost certainly cease of its own accord as the underlying psychological dis-ease is understood and eliminated.

Beware of *labelling* a child as a stammerer or stutterer, which is likely to perpetuate the problem.

(See also **Anxiety, Handicaps, Nervousness, Shyness.**)

Stealing

A child under the age of about six who steals should be presumed to do so because she is still morally inept – that is, she does not yet have a consolidated understanding of morality in general and/or that taking things belonging to other people, in particular, is morally taboo.

From six to twelve, a child's stealing should be understood as indicative of *serious emotional disturbance* (unless he has actually never been given moral exhortations to the contrary, in which case he has a serious charcter disorder leading inevitably to later criminality). A six- to twelve-year-old child who knows that to steal is 'wrong', and yet does so, probably does so out of a compulsive (although unconscious) bid to compensate for a void inside himself that should be filled with a secure feeling of being loved. While this may be a transient response to a current trauma in his life – such as the separation of his parents or the death of a family member – it should always be taken as a very loud cry for help by the child, and appropriate psychotherapeutic help sought.

From twelve to sixteen, stealing is very commonplace as one of the innumerable amoral or immoral ways through which a child – naturally at this stage – rebels against virtually *everything* that he perceives as characteristic of his parents, what they have taught him, and what they expect of him. While most morally upright parents are horrified to discover their pubescent child to be stealing, and quite rightly express their horror to the child, it is generally quite inappropriate for them to infer either that their child is seriously disturbed or that they have been seriously remiss in their upbringing of him. As in many other instances where pubescent rebelliousness goes beyond the limits of the parents' tolerance, and they firmly draw the line with appropriate outrage, the child is usually sufficiently ashamed and abashed that he is unlikely ever to do it again.

Over the age of sixteen, stealing is appropriately understood to be simply the immoral and illegal act we usually understand it to be. 'Kleptomania', however, acknowledges that it is possible, even in adult life, for stealing to be an emotional disorder rather than the character disorder it typically represents.

At any age, retributive punishment for stealing – or for any other immoral act – serves no positive purpose, and actually reinforces the impulse to behave similarly again. It is best to deal with developmentally normal stealing (*around puberty*) by demanding an explanation from the child as to 'How *could* you do such a thing?', implying that the child *is* essentially moral but that an impetuous impulse caused her to break her own moral code, for which she is now deeply ashamed. When parents respond this way to pubescent stealing, it is unlikely to occur more than once. Reparation must, of course, be taken for granted and insisted on.

(See also **Character, Delinquency, Lying, Morality, Punishment, Twelve to sixteen.**)

Step-children

The relationship between a child and his or her step-parent(s) is inevitably very difficult, and requires the utmost sensitivity and deep honesty on the part of all the grown-ups involved. The core issues are obedience and sexuality, and while most adults find it easy enough to be open about difficulties surrounding obedience, few are willing to be fully honest about the sexual issues.

Under the age of three a child is generally able and willing happily to accept a loving step-parent as a replacement for the parent he or she has lost. Such a child is likely to grow up experiencing the step-parent as if he or she were his or her natural parent.

After the age of three, acceptance by a child of a step-parent is only achieved by very careful and sensitive handling. Typically, a child lives with his or her mother and step-father, so what I have to say will apply to that situation, although for a child living with his or her father and step-mother the same comments will apply, but with symmetrical oppositeness, according to gender.

For a boy, from three to six and in adolescence, a step-father is a very valuable asset indeed, because the step-father denies him the psychologically tragic destiny of having his unconscious wish to 'possess' his mother fulfilled by having 'got rid of' his rivalrous father. Notwithstanding that a boy at these stages in his development is likely to make things as difficult as he can for his step-father, his step-father's insistent, 'I'm-more-powerful-than-you-and-don't-dare-talk-to-your-mother-like-that' attitude, combined with loving sharing of time with the boy in some exclusively masculine pursuits, provides assurance against the potentially devastating pathological relationship that could so easily otherwise develop between the boy and his single mother.

For a girl, from three to six and in adolescence, her relationship to her step-father is intrinsically unhealthy. For the child, her beloved father has been betrayed by her mother (however contrary are the objective facts), and she has lost the Oedipal battle – with a vengeance! She hates her mother for this and is ambivalently hateful and sexual towards her step-father. Having her father's love so cruelly wrenched from her (by his departure) and thus being implicitly humiliated by her mother, now that she is presented with a substitute for her father (in terms of authority), she seeks, quite understandably, to get her revenge on her mother and at the same time to repair her deeply damaged sexual self-esteem by courting her step-father. And, if she is an adolescent, the circumstances favour her revenge. She is, indeed, more nubile than her mother, and in her quest for her step-father's love, the incest taboo (which would protect her from too great an intimacy with her natural father) is absent. And her step-father, anyway, is uncomfortably aware of the sexual impulses he feels towards the child.

At worst, the relationship between an adolescent girl and her step-father becomes blatantly sexual, and the girl actually doubles the psychological problems she acquired when she lost her intimacy with her father. At best, mother, daughter, and step-father fend off the threatened disastrous outcomes of intimacy between the girl and her step-father with counter-active vehement anger and aggression flung out by all of them in all directions, but especially between the girl and her step-father.

All of this is diluted and mitigated if the step-father joined the family well before the girl reached puberty. But if the girl is over the age of twelve when she acquires her step-father, it is healthiest that, continuously and from the start, they have as close to a *non-relationship* as possible. The mother needs to tell her daughter, 'I am getting married again because I love this man very much. However, *you* don't have to love him – or even like him. He's not your father and won't, I promise you, try to act as if he is. All I ask is that you are reasonably polite to him.' The daughter will be deeply appreciative towards her mother for these explicit permissions and implicit directives that will protect her from unhappiness or trauma through the acquisition of a step-father.

Six to twelve is the least sexual stage in a child's development, so, for both boys and girls, the acquisition of a step-parent at this stage has the best chance of easy and wholesome adaptation for all those who are involved.

All of this may sound to some readers excessively psychoanalytic and not in keeping with their own observations of step-parent/step-children relationships that seem to function easily and well. However, I contend that all I have said is deeply true and is much better understood than glossed over, for the sake of the long-term emotional well-being of the children involved.

(See also **Custody, Divorce, Single parent.**)

Superstitions

See **Compulsions, God, Magic.**

Talking to strangers

Sadly, the world as we know it seems not to be as safe as it was a generation or so ago, when mothers generally left their babies and toddlers in prams and pushchairs outside shops, etc., without ever dreaming of their child being abducted. Now, parents are made acutely aware, through the media, of the very real possibilities of any child being molested or abducted by a stranger in even the 'safest' neighbourhoods. Now they feel the necessity to keep their babies and toddlers constantly in sight and to warn their children prohibitively concerning talking to strangers.

While it is undoubtedly true that the risks of molestation or abduction of a child are real, the statistical chances of his being harmed by a malevolent stranger still remain very small, compared, say, with the risk of accidents through carelessness, and especially compared with the risk of traffic accidents.

So while I endorse any parent's conscientious warnings given to her child about 'talking to strangers', I would urge her not to over-emphasize the risks and so induce in her child a general fearfulness of people. Warning, and occasionally reminding, a child never to *go* anywhere with a stranger because 'he might be a bad person who could hurt you' is quite sufficient. Don't deny your child the joy of *talking* to strangers and permission to assume the essential *goodness* of nearly everybody.

(See also **Good and evil, Protectiveness, Worrying about your child.**)

Teachers

In their role relationship with children, teachers are, by definition, *in loco parentis*, and are as entitled to the same degree of respectful obedience from your child as you are.

Never endorse any complaints your child makes to you about any of his teachers, which would be tantamount to your explicitly siding with your child against your child's other parent. This would be deeply traumatizing to the child and likely to produce in him a life-long propensity to form deeply unhappy 'triangular' relationships.

You may not always be entirely in agreement with what teachers instruct or demand of your child, but remember, your child 'belongs to' society as well as to you and your family, and teachers represent the 'parent' of society. If, nonetheless, you feel just cause to challenge the treatment of your child by one of his teachers, consult the teacher and/or the head teacher of the school. It is best not to tell your child you are going to see his teacher, but if you do mention to him that you are going, make sure your words and tone imply to him your expectation that you and his teacher will seek and find *agreement* concerning what is best for him.

(See also **Protectiveness, Quarrelling, School.**)

Teasing

Teasing is a way of expressing love ironically. That is, under the disguise of being critical, a tease is actually expressing affection for the very characteristics he or she is manifestly taunting the other for. Some people enjoy being teased; others hate it. Broadly speaking, children (and adults) who enjoy being teased are those who are somewhat emotionally inhibited, and find it difficult to receive love too obviously given. Children (and adults) who hate being teased are those, on the same broad terms, who have a nervous disposition, and demand a great deal of explicit love from others. Be aware of and respect such differences in your children.

(See also **Temperament.**)

Temperament

Temperament (as contrasted with character) is innate and, by and large, immutable. In many families it is easy to observe that, when the parents are of markedly different temperaments, one child may clearly inherit the father's temperament, another the mother's.

Sometimes people of markedly different temperaments are very attractive to each other; sometimes they dislike each other. Often, people of similar temperament choose each other as friends; but sometimes they profoundly irritate each other. Be sensitive to your child's temperament and *enjoy her for the type of person she naturally is*, even if, in her temperamental differences from you, you find it hard to identify with her. Some of the unhappiest grown-ups are those who feel themselves to be innately 'bad' because their parents obviously disliked their temperaments.

(See also **Loneliness, Teasing.**)

Temper-tantrums

A temper-tantrum is a bid by one person to get from another, through violence, what the other does not want to give him or her. A spoilt person of any age will be inclined to temper-tantrums, although in grown-ups they are usually called 'having hysterics'. Temper-tantrums are to be expected at least occasionally from psychologically healthy, unspoilt children, especially at those stages of development when obedience is a core issue, namely one to three and twelve to sixteen.

The appropriate response by a parent to a temper-tantrum in a child is firm and loving control. The temper-tantrum must not be allowed to win for the child what he or she has been refused. Ideally, the parent should never relent and give the child what he or she demands, even *after* the temper-tantrums has subsided.

As soon as a child begins to have a temper-tantrum a parent should say something along the lines, 'I don't want to be with you when you are like this', and remove herself from the child's presence (or remove him physically from her presence, no matter how much he kicks), and *absolutely ignore the child until he stops*. However, it is important for the child not to experience this as abandonment or to infer that 'Mummy doesn't love me any more', so it helps if the parent adds, 'When you stop screaming, come to Mummy and I'll give you a cuddle.' If the child stops screaming, comes for a cuddle, and while being cuddled starts the temper-tantrum again, repeat the separation of the child from your presence and repeat the whole process as before. A child so treated will very rarely have temper-tantrums.

Some parents are able to respond well to their child's temper-tantrums at home, but not in public where they feel embarrassed in the face of other people's apparent disapproval that they are not responding to the screaming of their child. However, notwithstanding that, in public, a parent cannot remove herself from her child, I urge her to abide by the general principle of ignoring the child, rather than smacking him or in any other way deferring to what she believes *other people* think she should do.

Temper-tantrums become inculcated as a chronic response to frustration in the child when a parent *tries hard* to resist giving into the temper-tantrum and sometimes succeeds and sometimes does not. Thus, for example, if a mother ignores a child's temper-tantrum for ten minutes and then can stand it no more and so gives in to his demand for a chocolate biscuit or whatever, the next time the child starts a temper-tantrum he will go on for *at least ten minutes*. He will be saying to himself (even if unconsciously), 'I've got to keep this up for ten minutes, because, from past experience, I know she can resist me for as long as this, but then she gives in.' In this way the child can learn to keep up his temper-tantrums for longer and longer stretches at a time, and the deconditioning process becomes ever harder. If a parent doubts her ability to resist her child's temper-tantrums, it is far better to give in immediately than to hold out for as long as she can bear it, and then give in. When a parent who has always quickly given in to a temper-tantrum commits herself to not doing so any more, the process of deconditioning takes a very short time.

The appropriate treatment for temper-tantrums is also the appropriate treatment for *any* behaviour in a child (or adult) that a parent (or anybody) wants to stop. In a nutshell: give in quickly, every time, while you doubt your willpower *absolutely* to resist; once you are determined to put an end to the behaviour, *never again* give in to it (even though you will have to resist even worse and more prolonged temper-tantrums for a while as the child 'fights back' against your resistance); and, above all else, *never resist for a while and then give in.*

(See also **Aggression, Control, Discipline, Firmness, Frustration, Permissiveness, Prohibitions, Punishment, Reasoning.**)

Threats

Threats are a heavy-handed and flat-footed way of negotiating. Prefer bribery. *If you do choose to use threats, never fail to carry them out*, otherwise you will become an object of derision to your child, lose all control over her, will be seen to be a liar by her, and invite her to become a liar too.

(See also **Bribery, Control, Discipline, Emotions (parental), Firmness, Permissions, Prohibitions, Punishment, Truthfulness.**)

Thumb-sucking

See **Habits, Regression.**

Tidiness

Nearly all children are inclined chronically to be more untidy than their parents wish them to be. A child is naturally likely to be her tidiest self from six to twelve and her untidiest self from twelve to sixteen. The truth of the matter is that tidiness is *not* a moral matter, even though parents often demand it of their children as if it were. Especially from twelve to sixteen, moral exhortations to the child concerning tidiness are likely to be entirely ineffective, because not only is the child naturally extremely rebellious at this stage but she also sees straight through the lie. That is, she may be *somewhat* inclined not to steal, cheat, or lie, even at this stage, because she still has *some* respect for morality, but she knows tidiness is not a moral matter and so she rebels against her parents' demands for it with an utterly clear conscience.

Tidiness is actually simply the parents' preference – like, for example, their preference for blue carpet or eating dinner promptly at 7 o'clock. If the parents are honest enough to acknowledge this they are much more likely to elicit at least some cooperation by negotiation – even from a twelve- to sixteen-year-old, who may feel just sufficient goodwill towards her parents to respond positively to, 'I know it doesn't matter to you, but it would make me very happy indeed if you tidied up your room', or 'I'll make a deal with you: if you tidy up your room this morning, I'll buy you that new pair of jeans I promised you this afternoon or give you fifty pence for every plastic bag you fill with rubbish.'

(See also **Bribery.**)

Timidity

Timidity is unnecessary fearfulness. It may be an innate characteristic of a child's temperament or a consequence of parental over-protectiveness, or a mixture of both. *Never* brutalize a child by forcing or tricking him into doing whatever it is he fears. Rather, gently reassure and coax him, give him permission to overcome his fears by your own enthusiastic fearlessness, and offer him generous bribes.

(See also **Bribery, Fear, Good and evil, Permission, Protectiveness, Temperament.**)

Toilet training

See **Potty training.**

Truthfulness

Truthfulness is an aspect of character, and is therefore *taught* by explicit moral exhortation. But it is also a permission, and is therefore also *learnt implicitly* by a child from the truthfulness of her parents. Don't expect your child to be more truthful with you than you are with her!

When truthfulness has been both given as a permission to a child and also taught, and yet the child is untruthful, the reason is likely to be either that the child fears the consequences of the truth or that the child is defending herself against your intrusion into the *privacy* of thought and feeling that she is entitled to – just as you are. If you truthfully tell your child that you don't want to tell her about some things that you feel entitled to be private about, so will she equally truthfully tell you when she prefers to maintain her privacy, which – especially from puberty onwards – should be respected.

(See also **Character, Fantasy, Lying, Modesty, Permissions.**)

Violence

See **Aggression, Fighting.**

Vegetarianism

Voluntary vegetarianism on moral or political grounds is fashionable at present in our society, and so often appeals to pubescent children. For them it fulfils the joint aims of finding a focus for their burgeoning moral and political idealism, (righteously) rebelling against their (carnivorous) parents' way of life, and finding security of conformity in their anti-conformity!

Respect your child's idealism but insist that she takes vitamin B supplements (which he or she will definitely need, even if vegetarian adults do not).

Beware, though, of your child embracing vegetarianism for what she claims to be health reasons. If, despite your assurances that meat will do her no harm, your child absolutely insists on maintaining her stance, take this as a sign that the child may be quite seriously ill at ease about life itself. This dis-ease should be uncovered and cured.

(See also **Anorexia Nervosa, Eating.**)

Wakefulness

Most children are more wakeful than their parents wish them to be, and are willing to go to bed later and wake up earlier than their parents wish they would. However, the obverse applies to teenagers, who typically irritate their parents by their unwillingness to get up until afternoon. Both wakefulness in early childhood and slothful sleepiness from puberty onwards are absolutely normal developmentally.

However, wakefulness in a child associated with his obvious tiredness during the day suggests some psychological dis-ease pertaining to going to sleep that needs to be discovered, understood, and overcome. Quite commonly, such wakefulness is a bid on the part of the child to fulfil his need for more loving attention from his parents than he is currently getting.

(See also **Sleep problems.**)

Whining

The whining of a child is utterly irritating to parents, although between the ages of about one and three it needs to be accepted as a transition between crying as the child's only means of communicating her needs, to full verbal articulateness about her feelings and desires. Whining should be discouraged by parents' refusals to grant anything asked for this way. Ready fulfilment (as often as possible and appropriate) should be made of the child's desires if they are expressed in a *non*-whining, polite way.

Spoilt children whine most.

(See also **Clingingness, Spoiling.**)

Working mothers

It has become the case in recent years that very often it takes two wage earners in a family to pay the mortgage and generally make ends meet. As a result, many mothers have no option but to go out to work very soon after their babies are born. Sad as this situation is in denying a mother the fulfilment of her natural instinct to be the primary caretaker of her young child, this does not mean that her child will suffer as long as it has somebody to whom it can become healthily attached, through that person's utter reliability and sufficient nurturing attention.

(See also **Child care, Separation.**)

Worrying about your child

Worrying about somebody is not, as it pretends to be, loving, but is actually an insidiously hateful attitude that imposes on the person worried about both a fear for their own well-being and a huge burden of helpless guilt towards the worrier for the clinging symbiosis of the relationship.

At an unconscious level a person who chronically worries about another actually wishes the feared disaster on the person he or she worries about even though – and indeed because – the relationship is *too* close and *too* loving. That is, the worrier actually resents the dependence of the worried-about person. The chronic worrier is somebody whose own dependency needs have not been appropriately and adequately met in childhood, and he or she defends against the pain of herself not having been loved enough by the 'compensation' of drawing to and keeping in bondage needily dependent others.

Now children *are* symbiotically dependent on their parents, and there are inevitably times when even the healthiest parents resent the reality that so often they have to forego their own needs and desires in favour of lovingly nourishing the needs and desires of their children. And there *are* occasions when the child's well-being and safety are legitimately a cause of worry to the parents, especially at puberty, when the child begins to make necessarily wild and pre-emptive bids for separation from the safety of his parents' care and control. But a loving parent, having set appropriate limits on the child's freedom, must accept that some risk-taking on the part of the child must be allowed and must be borne by the parents as best they can.

Of course you are going to lie awake worrying when your fifteen-year-old daughter said she would be home by midnight and she is still not in by one-thirty. But when she finally does come in, do not jump out of bed and confront her with, 'I've been worried sick . . . etc.' Rather, pretend to be asleep, and in the morning say, 'I don't know what time you got in, but I woke up at half-past one and you weren't here, and you said you would be home by midnight. I know you are very capable of looking after yourself, and I trust you, but you know people *do* get mugged and assaulted, however grown-up they are, and I am entitled to your consideration for my natural concern for your safety. It's got nothing to do with your age. Everybody should have the consideration to be reliable towards the people who love them and may be concerned for their safety. From now on, if anything prevents you getting home when you thought you would, I expect you to let me know *before* I expect you, or else to leave a telephone number where I can contact you and find out that you're OK, so I can happily go to sleep.'

What you thus induce in the child is genuine loving consideration for your feelings, rather than fearful apprehension about her ability to look after herself, combined with resentful guilt towards you for the cloying and deeply damaging imposition on her of your worry.

(See also **Independence, Protectiveness, Safety.**)

INDEX

*Page numbers in **bold** denote a main entry in the A–Z section*

Twelve to sixteen—*contd*
119, 129, 136, 138, and see
Puberty

Unconscious mind *vi, 29, 48, 51,
84, 98, 114, 126, 129, 130, 137,
142*
Under-achieving *55*
'Unfinished business' *84–5*

Values *19, 38, 53, 153*
Vegetarianism **140**
Viciousness *14, 62*
Violence *14, 57, 136, and see*
Aggression, Fighting
Violence between parents *57*

Vulnerability *13, 16, 54, 55, 60,
61, 75, 77, 79, 81, 100, 101, 112,
119, 120, 121*

Wakefulness **141**
Walking to school *110*
Washing hands *112*
Wasting (money) *91*
Whining **141**
'White lies' *11, 87*
Withdrawal *52*
Working mothers **142**
Worrying about your child **142–3**
Worrying by your child *33*

Youngest child *33–4, 128*